Frontispiece Jacques Lecoq (1989)

JACQUES LECOQ

Routledge Performance Practitioners is a series of introductory guides to the key theatre-makers of the last century. Each volume explains the background to and the work of one of the major influences on twentieth- and twenty-first-century performance.

Jacques Lecoq's influence on the theatre of the latter half of the twentieth century cannot be overestimated. This is the first book to combine:

- an historical introduction to his life and the context in which he worked
- an analysis of his teaching methods and principles of body work, movement, creativity and contemporary theatre
- detailed studies of the work of Théâtre de Complicité and Mummenschanz
- practical exercises demonstrating Lecoq's distinctive approach to actor training.

As a first step towards critical understanding, and as an initial exploration before going on to further, primary research, **Routledge Performance Practitioners** are unbeatable value for today's student.

Simon Murray (stage name for Simon Henderson) is a senior lecturer in theatre and performance at the University of Sunderland. He has been a professional performer and director in the field of physical and visual theatre.

ROUTLEDGE PERFORMANCE PRACTITIONERS

Series editor: Franc Chamberlain, University of Northampton

Routledge Performance Practitioners is an innovative series of introductory handbooks on key figures in twentieth-century performance practice. Each volume focuses on a theatre-maker whose practical and theoretical work has in some way transformed the way we understand theatre and performance. The books are carefully structured to enable the reader to gain a good grasp of the fundamental elements underpinning each practitioner's work. They will provide an inspiring springboard for future study, unpacking and explaining what can initially seem daunting.

The main sections of each book will cover:

* personal biography
* explanation of key writings
* description of significant productions
* reproduction of practical exercises.

The first volumes of the series are:

Michael Chekhov by Franc Chamberlain
Jacques Lecoq by Simon Murray
Vsevolod Meyerhold by Jonathan Pitches
Konstantin Stanislavsky by Bella Merlin

Future volumes will include:

Eugenio Barba
Pina Bausch
Augusto Boal
Bertolt Brecht
Peter Brook
Jerzy Grotowski
Anna Halprin
Joan Littlewood
Ariane Mnouchkine

JACQUES LECOQ

Simon Murray

Routledge
Taylor & Francis Group

LONDON AND NEW YORK

First published 2003
by Routledge
2 Park Square, Milton Park, Abingdon, Oxon OX14 4RN

Simultaneously published in the USA and Canada
by Routledge
711 Third Avenue, New York, NY 10017

Routledge is an imprint of the Taylor & Francis Group

Typeset in Perpetua by
Florence Production Ltd, Stoodleigh, Devon
Printed and bound in Great Britain by
CPI Antony Rowe, Chippenham, Wiltshire

British Library Cataloguing in Publication Data
A catalogue record for this book is available from
the British Library

Library of Congress Cataloging in Publication Data
Murray, Simon David, 1948–
    Jacques Lecoq / Simon David Murray.
      p. cm. – (Routledge performance practitioners)
    Includes bibliographical references and index.
    1. Lecoq, Jacques – Criticism and interpretation.
    I. Title.   II. Series.
    PN2638.L349M87 2003
    792'.028'092 – sc21   2003004052

ISBN 978-0-415-25881-4 (hbk)
ISBN 978-0-415-25882-1 (pbk)

FOR WENDY AND ISLA
AND IN MEMORY OF
PETER, PAM AND IRIS

CONTENTS

FIGURES

ACKNOWLEDGEMENTS

My thanks go most particularly to Fay Lecoq, Pascale Lecoq, Thomas Prattki and Rita Leys at the École Internationale de Théâtre Jacques Lecoq in Paris. I visited the Lecoq school on five occasions when researching and writing the book and each time Fay was enormously patient and helpful with my numerous requests and questions. I especially valued the access she provided for me to view material from the school's video and photographic archive, and for sitting beside me when watching *Tout bouge* (and other recorded material) to translate when my own French was found wanting. I hope very much that this book does justice to the memory of her late husband, and to his remarkable work in theatre. Pascale talked to me with great passion and insight about Laboratoire d'Étude du Mouvement (LEM) and allowed me to watch classes and the final presentation of work in June 2002. Rita's help around the school's photographic archive, in facilitating my choice of images for the book and in tracing some of the photographers, was greatly appreciated. Thomas, who has now left Paris after teaching with Jacques Lecoq for nearly ten years, was extraordinarily generous in giving me his time for a number of fascinating conversations about the school and its daily practice, philosophy and history. The chapter presenting practical exercises could not have been written without his collaboration and perceptive advice. Finally, here, I must thank Fay and her children – as executors of the Lecoq estate – for allowing me to use translated extracts from *Le Théâtre du geste*.

I would also like to thank David Bradby, Andy Crook, Dick McCaw, John Keefe and Mark Evans for agreeing to talk to me in some depth about their various experiences of Jacques Lecoq. Our conversations were vital in helping to shape and refine what has been written here, and I valued highly their wisdom and humour in responding to my awkward questions. In addition, Mark gave me invaluable advice and information on the work of the elusive Georges Hébert, for which many thanks.

I must thank Bernie Schürch and Floriana Frassetto, founder members of Mummenschanz, for offering me the opportunity to visit Switzerland in a heat wave. Our conversation about the company's work and Bernie's experience of being at the Paris school in 1968 was invaluable and informative. These interviews and other aspects of the research were made possible by a grant from the Arts and Humanities Research Board (AHRB) and I am most grateful to the AHRB for supporting the project in this way.

Thanks must also go to performing arts colleagues at the University of Sunderland and, before that, at the University College of Ripon and York St John for indulging the preoccupations and obsessions which gave rise to this book, and in supporting me when I took time away from teaching for research and writing. I am grateful to the following students from the University of Sunderland who dragged themselves away from their scholarship to look at a section of the manuscript and offer perceptive comments, particularly on the clarity of my writing style: Jason Savin, Harmony Gears, Laura Smith, Jeremy Hodgson and Fieona McCabe.

Gill Kester did a most imaginative, skilful and expert job in translating essays from *Le Théâtre du geste*. I am indebted to Gill for the time and energy that she devoted to this and other translating tasks. Franc Chamberlain, the series editor, and Talia Rodgers from Routledge have been great in answering my naive questions, and for generally giving me support and advice throughout the process. Thanks to both of them. In various ways, and perhaps without knowing it, the following have helped me in the process of thinking about Jacques Lecoq, researching his work and composing the book: Alan Clarke, Claire Hobbs, Toni Lunn, Marilynne Davies, Mark Batty, Paul Harman, Sally Madge, John Quinn, Paula Turner, Jo Kendall and Eline van de Voort.

Many of the images reproduced here were selected from the Lecoq school's considerable photographic archive and I am very grateful to

Fay Lecoq for giving me access to this treasure. I must thank Mummenschanz for allowing me to use some striking photographs of the company's work over a thirty-year period, and to the following photographers who gave me authority to use images that I had found within the Lecoq archive: Richard and Patrick Lecoq, Liliane de Kermadec, Michèle Laurent, Alain Chambaretaud, Justin Case, Pia Zanatti and the estate of the late Robert Doisneau. Scott Heist, a professional photographer from North America, has himself produced a photo essay on Jacques Lecoq and I must particularly thank Scott for allowing me access to his work, and for being especially helpful in debating options with me. I hope our burgeoning cross-Atlantic e-mail friendship will continue. Despite considerable and varied attempts to trace other photographers whose images I have used in the book, I was unable to find any way of contacting the following: Enger, Venlo and Ferruccio Fantini.

My friend, the performer, writer and Lecoq graduate, Alan Fairbairn, has continuously amused me on this particular journey, but also offered sound and serious advice when it was most needed. Finally, enormous and incalculable thanks to Wendy for being there, and for cajoling and supporting me – intellectually and emotionally – through flaky moments, and to my daughter Isla who has so often diverted me through her laughter and demands for *play*.

NOTE ON TEXT AND ILLUSTRATIONS

I have provided a name glossary of selected figures – largely from the world of theatre – who feature in the text. Inclusion in the glossary is indicated by the name in question being printed in bold on its first appearance in the script. The glossary is deliberately selective and excludes better known names such as Brecht, Artaud and Stanislavsky, assuming the reader's acquaintance with these luminaries. However, it also excludes people who, although not well known – Amletto Sartori and Étienne Decroux, for example – have had their work discussed in the main body of the text.

From time to time I have also offered brief definitions – or commentaries – of selected terms which can give rise to uncertainty and confusion. These are 'boxed' and the term is indicated in bold print on its first mention in the text.

I have tried wherever possible to use the third person plural pronoun (their). However, there are times – particularly in the 'Practical exercises' chapter – when the sense I was trying to convey made this clumsy or inappropriate. Here, I have had to use 'he', 'his' or 'him' on occasions. In these circumstances 'he' etc. should always be construed as being either male or female. In the 'Practical exercises' chapter I have quite often used direct address – 'you' (i.e. the student) – in order to provide a more immediate and informal mode of communication. This convention does not occur in the rest of the book.

I gratefully acknowledge the following copyright holders for the use of their photographs: Frontispiece, Patrick Lecoq; Figure 1.1, Liliane de Kermadec; Figure 1.2, Ferruccio Fantini; Figure 1.3, Justin Case; Figure 1.4, Robert Doisneau; Figure 1.5, Liliane de Kermadec; Figure 1.6, Venlo; Figure 2.1, Richard Lecoq; Figure 2.2, Patrick Lecoq; Figure 2.3, H. Scott Heist 03/Splinter Cottage from *My Observations of Jacques Lecoq*; Figure 2.4, Liliane de Kermadec; Figure 2.5, Enger; Figure 2.6, Enger; Figure 2.7, Michèle Laurent; Figure 2.8, Justin Case; Figures 3.1–4, Mummenschanz/Zanatti; Figure 5.1, Alain Chambaretaud.

THE LIFE OF
JACQUES LECOQ

A theatre school should not always journey in the wake of existing theatre forms. On the contrary, it should have a visionary aspect, developing new languages of the stage and thus assisting in the renewal of theatre itself.

(Lecoq 2000: 162)

JACQUES LECOQ (1921–99)

When Jacques Lecoq died in 1999, world theatre lost one of its most imaginative, influential and pioneering thinkers and teachers. Compared to many of the figures featured in this series, little has yet been written about Jacques Lecoq. While this can be partly explained by that phenomenon common to many great artistic and cultural innovators of not being fully recognised until after their death, it is also because Lecoq is celebrated almost exclusively as a teacher and thinker, rather than for plays he might have written or for the productions he directed and choreographed.

Jacques Lecoq's real influence lies embodied within thousands of performers, writers, movement choreographers and theatre directors across the world who were once his students in Paris – and elsewhere – during a period of forty-two years. To a greater or lesser extent, his *signature* rests inscribed in the theatre these 'students' have constructed, in the performances they have made and in the plays they have written or directed. This book attempts to bring that *signature* into sharper focus by offering responses to the following sorts of questions. Who was Jacques Lecoq? What did he do? Why was his work important? How did his thinking and practice connect to other significant figures of twentieth-century theatre? Why is his legacy *still* important for contemporary theatre?

The first part of this chapter attempts to paint a picture of Lecoq's life in France and Italy from the end of the Second World War, tracing his development as actor, director, movement choreographer and theatre teacher. Following this early history, I examine the foundations of the Paris school and consider its organisation and structure. The rest of this chapter considers the broader historical and cultural context into which Lecoq's life and work may helpfully be placed and understood. Conventional wisdom suggests that, historically, Lecoq's legacy from Jacques Copeau (1879–1949) was the definitive influence that most shaped and framed his work. However, in so far as Lecoq ever chose to invoke other twentieth-century theatre practitioners as sources of authority, the figure of Antonin Artaud (1896–1948) should be equally acknowledged. Here, I focus on Copeau, while arguing that what primarily drove Lecoq was not some kind of self-conscious attempt to place himself within any particular tradition of European theatre, but an overriding curiosity with the body and how it moved. Having speculated about historical influences, I then consider the recent dramatic rise – in Britain and parts of Europe – of theatre forms which foreground the performer's body and its movement in space, and reflect on Lecoq's role in these developments. Finally, in continuing an attempt to locate his work upon a bigger cultural canvas, a brief account is offered of the ways in which the human body has become a central concern in other disciplines apparently unconnected to theatre and performance. This whole chapter provides a framework which the subsequent three parts of the book will flesh out and substantiate through:

1 a detailed, but selective analysis of Lecoq's writing;
2 analytical and discursive case studies of the work of two companies which acknowledge the importance of his training for their creative work; and
3 a sequence of practical exercises designed to capture and illustrate some essential principles and characteristics of Lecoq's teaching at the Paris school.

To think about the life and work of Lecoq; to understand the how, what and why of fifty years of pedagogy; to consider his theorising on how *things*, materials, humans . . . animals move; to reflect upon his ideas on how performance communicates itself; to debate his views on theatre's stake in the politics of place, identity and internationalism is to engage with issues utterly germane to the problems and challenges of contemporary theatre practice. This is a book about how one of Western Europe's great teachers of theatre, working in the second half of the twentieth century, implicitly and explicitly presented a challenge to much of the received wisdom on actor training and – hence – the making of contemporary performance.

To put it another way, Lecoq is important to our understanding of contemporary Western drama because he was a central figure in a loose movement of practitioners, teachers and theorists who proposed that it is the actor's body – rather than simply the spoken text – which is the crucial generator of meaning(s) in theatre. Lecoq's school in Paris thrived (and, at the time of writing, continues to flourish) during a period when many young European theatre-makers were creating work which they – or the publicity departments of theatres and arts centres – wished to describe as *physical theatre*, *movement theatre*, *body-based theatre*, *visual performance*, or even occasionally *modern mime*. Whether these labels help us to understand a particular theatrical form is debatable. Nonetheless, there can be little doubt – especially within Britain – that, from the 1970s, there was a significant increase in the amount of devised performance which emphasised movement, gesture and mime as the main expressive tools of theatre. That this development was particularly marked in Britain reflects a reaction against a dominant tradition which has given an almost deferential authority to the playwright in the construction of theatre – a tradition that has placed the *spoken word* at the centre of the theatrical experience, and one that, arguably, has been more pronounced in Britain than in other countries of Europe. Translated into actual live performance this has been a theatre culture that applauded and celebrated actors with a rich vocal range and virtuosity which often, however, far exceeded their talent or aptitude for expressive movement and gesture. Many British drama schools offering training for the aspiring professional actor have consciously reinforced this perspective by prioritising vocal expertise at the expense of other physical skills within their curricula.

The reasons for the upsurge in forms of theatre which have privileged the expressive potential of the actor's body are complex, and cannot simply and unproblematically be reduced to the influence of those theatre practitioners and teachers who also chose to explore the power of movement and gesture as tools of communication on stage. While Jacques Lecoq and his contemporaries, such as **Jerzy Grotowski** (1933–99), **Eugenio Barba** (1936–), **Peter Brook** (1925–) and Étienne Decroux (1898–1991), have all had a major impact on the shape and direction of what one might wish to call 'body-based' theatre in the West since the 1950s, to understand their work fully it is necessary to consider the wider cultural movements within which their own specific practice existed.

The significance of the body in late twentieth-century Western culture goes well beyond the performing arts and permeates the discourses of – for example – cultural studies, sociology, psychology, anthropology and feminist theory. It is not the place of this book to examine those wider cultural forces that provide a framework for theatre movements celebrating movement and physicality, although much of what follows implicitly engages with these broader issues.

So, if Jacques Lecoq is but a single player in a larger pattern of cultural circumstances all concerned with the significance of the *body*, he is nonetheless a very considerable one within the field of contemporary theatre and performance. His influence on a wider debate about actor training and the meaning of movement and physical expression within theatre has been substantial. However, his impact on the *actual* production of theatre and approaches to performing in Western cultures over the last thirty years has been equally significant, though perhaps less straightforward to detect. The roll-call of directors, writers and actors who at one time trained with Lecoq is extensive. Among the better known we may identify: Philippe Avron, Luc Bondy, Michel Azama, Yasmina Réza, Steven Berkoff, **Ariane Mnouchkine** (1939–), Geoffrey Rush and **Julie Taymor** (1952–). Of the companies which have acknowledged a collective debt to Lecoq, the most significant include: Théâtre de Complicité, Mummenschanz, Footsbarn, Théâtre du Soleil, Moving Picture Mime Show, Els Joglars and Els Comediants.

The issues with which any investigation into the work of Jacques Lecoq must engage, and which this book attempts to examine and analyse, may be summarised as follows:

- Play and the creative actor
- The performer's body and the generation of meaning(s)
- Bodies: culturally inscribed or universally constructed?
- The subversive clown, *bouffon* or grotesque
- Matter: texture, movement, sound and taste
- Rapport and *complicité* in the creation of ensemble
- Preparing the body for theatre
- Mime and nature: mime and theatre
- Internationalism, humanism and theatre
- Connecting two centuries: the legacy of the modernist avant-garde
- Against interpretation: the practitioner as art form
- Space, architecture, mobility and stillness
- Releasing mime from the closet
- Mask and anti-mask: from neutrality to the red nose.

LECOQ, GROTOWSKI AND OTHER BODIES

Jacques Lecoq died on 19 January 1999. By one of those strange coincidences of timing which invite us to reflect on the cultural forces that frame and shape artistic innovation and development, the Polish teacher and theorist of actor training, Jerzy Grotowski, had died only five days earlier. Although their approaches to the training of actors differed in many significant respects – and there seems little evidence that either invoked the other in his writing or teaching – these major figures of twentieth-century European theatre are connected in at least two significant ways. First, they were both deeply influenced by a way of looking at actor training initiated through the radical experiments of the French theatre director, Jacques Copeau. For Grotowski, the link was through Copeau's nephew, **Michel Saint-Denis** (1897–1971), whom he called 'my spiritual father'. For Lecoq, the connection is by virtue of his 'apprenticeship' to **Jean Dasté** (1904–94), Copeau's son-in-law. Second – and crucially – is their joint insistence that the creative 'pulse' at the heart of theatre is the actor's body, its movement and its stillness. For Copeau, Grotowski and Lecoq – but in varying ways – it is the actor's body that is both starting and finishing point of all live performance. Such an apparently unexceptional observation – shared by other significant theatre practitioners – however, disguises often contesting assumptions about what the body actually is, and whether through theatre training it can be stripped of all its cultural habits and dispositions acquired through socialisation. Arguably, the body of the performer and its ability to generate 'presence' and/or to 'represent' authentically has been the most significant challenge for Western theatre-makers over the last three decades. At the same time, this issue – how the performing body is constructed and communicates itself – has perhaps been the central problematic facing academics of theatre and performance studies. As this book attempts to illustrate, the work and thinking of Jacques Lecoq lie at the heart of such debates.

Although he was a prolific movement choreographer and director of plays between 1948 and 1956, while working and living in Italy, Lecoq's impact on world theatre, from the inauguration of his Paris school in 1956 until his death forty-three years later, can only really be measured *directly* through his teaching, research and occasional forays into writing. Almost all the other key figures of European (and American) **modernism** whose work has interrogated the theory and practice of acting – from Stanislavsky (1863–1938), **Vsevolod Meyerhold** (1874–1940), Copeau, Bertolt Brecht (1898–1956) and **Michael Chekhov** (1891–1955), through to Grotowski, **Joseph Chaikin** (1935–), Brook and Barba – have *also* directed, devised or choreographed work for the stage.

For practitioners such as these, teaching and research existed alongside directing and making professional theatre. For them, explorations into the nature of acting have been partly realised through the theatre productions for which they have been responsible. To the extent that such work has been documented – and within the considerable limitations which any documentation of live performance, however sensitive and sophisticated, places on the suspect notion of a single 'accurate record' – we can at least see or read about what apparently happened

---

Modernism is a complex historical and cultural phenomenon that embraces a wide – and often contradictory – range of ways of thinking about and explaining the world. Linked historically, but elastically, to a period from the late nineteenth to the mid-twentieth century, modernism embraces a wide variety of political, cultural and artistic movements which shared little other than a belief that nothing is as it seems, and that appearance and meaning have an awkward relationship with each other.

> **Mise-en-scène** means literally – from the French – the 'action of putting on the play'. It refers to all elements of the staging of a piece of theatre – lighting, design, props and costumes – and their relationship to each other and to spectators.
>
> **Dramaturgy** is the process of thinking about – and realising in practice – the appropriate theatrical vocabularies and languages for carrying the meanings of the piece to spectators. Dramaturgy or 'looking with knowledge' (Keefe 1995: 12) engages with the process of considering all the possible texts for a work of theatre and how these will fit together to shape the structure of the piece in question. 'The specific link between form and content' (Pavis 1998: 125).

on stage. Here, it is theoretically possible to unravel the connections between pedagogy, **dramaturgy**, *mise-en-scène* and performance.

For Lecoq, given that his experience of directing theatre in Italy chronologically *predates* forty-three years of theorising, research and practice-through-teaching at the Paris school, we have no such opportunity. What we do have instead is a shadowy legacy of the traces left by those companies and actors who trained with Lecoq and who will readily invoke his influence when their work is described, analysed and assessed. Chapter 3 of this book is devoted to considering the work of two companies – Mummenschanz and Théâtre de Complicité – many of whose actors trained at the Paris school. By focusing on these companies we are presented with the opportunity of tracing where and how Lecoq's influence is manifest through, for example, approaches to acting, deployment of dramatic space, manipulation of props and other objects and – above all – in a conscious devotion to the power of movement and gesture.

JACQUES LECOQ: ACTOR, DIRECTOR AND TEACHER

EARLY CAREER: FOUNDATIONS IN FRANCE AND ITALY (1940–56)

Jacques Lecoq was born in Paris in 1921. He was active in a variety of sports at school and throughout his life retained an interest in the way athletes effectively organise and use their bodies. At the age of twenty Lecoq attended a college of physical education at Bagatelle in the Paris suburbs and began to teach physical education, as well as coaching athletes to swim. At the college he met Jean-Marie Conty, an inter-national basketball player who was in charge of France's policy on physical education. Conty also had a strong interest in theatre and later set up a school entitled L'Éducation par le Jeu Dramatique (Education through Dramatic Performance). Here, in 1947, Lecoq was to teach classes on physical expression.

By the end of the Second World War he had started to undertake rehabilitation work among the disabled: 'he saw how a man with paral-ysis could organise his body in order to walk, and taught him to do so' (McBurney 1999a). Between 1945 and moving to Italy in 1948 Lecoq made his first connections with a number of theatre practitioners and teachers who provided a link back down the twentieth century to the pioneering work of Jacques Copeau and his laboratory for the renewal of French theatre and acting at L'École du Vieux Columbier. Lecoq's connections to the various 'technical' traditions that have shaped contemporary mime and movement theatre will be explored later in this section, but at this juncture we should note that the four key figures of twentieth-century French mime – **Jean-Louis Barrault** (1910–94), Étienne Decroux, **Marcel Marceau** (1923–) and Lecoq himself – can all trace their artistic lineage back to the teaching and thinking of Copeau in the 1920s. While this heritage is neither uncom-plicated, nor a simple affirmation of Copeau's legacy, various writers on modern mime and movement theatre – Myra Felner (1985), Tom Leabhart (1989) and Anthony Frost and Ralph Yarrow (1990) – have all noted the interconnected and 'incestuous' nature of the French mime tradition.

Shortly after the liberation of France, Lecoq joined the Association Travail et Culture (TEC). This was an influential organisation that, during the war, had served as the cultural wing of the French Resistance movement and had the purpose of opening up opportunities in artistic activities for working-class people. Frost and Yarrow note that TEC 'gave shows and organised spectacles for 10–15,000 people . . . echoes here of Fo and Piscator' (Frost and Yarrow 1990: 61). Here, Lecoq received his first formal theatre training and began to explore 'mimed improvisations' (Lecoq 2000: 4) with members of the company, a number of whom had been pupils of **Charles Dullin** (1885–1949).

> **Somatic** means relating to the body and implies an activity, or a process which is 'hands on' and physical rather than cerebral and intellectual. The term can sometimes unwittingly reinforce a false distinction between 'mind' and 'body'.

Dullin had also been a member of Copeau's first company, but set up his own studio for theatre research (the Atelier) in the 1930s. It was in the Atelier that Decroux and Barrault initiated their years of **somatic** 'research' into corporeal expression and thus laid the foundations for a codified grammar of mime that many years later Lecoq was himself to reject as too constricting. Lecoq records that, at the Association Travail et Culture, he performed:

> in Chartres to celebrate the return of prisoners of war . . . and in Grenoble where we participated in two large celebrations: one for the liberation of the city, and the other for the May Day holiday in honour of the work taken up again by men who had been liberated at last.
>
> (Lecoq 1987: 108)

It is interesting to surmise at this point the extent to which the young Lecoq's involvement in 'popular theatre' subsequently shaped the form and direction of his pedagogy at the Paris school until his death in 1999. The emphasis which many Lecoq disciples give to comic performance and clowning – at least in the early stages of their careers – seems to reflect a concern with the popular and accessible in theatre. David Bradby, translator of *The Moving Body* and writer on French theatre, regards this commitment as a significant indicator of the school's future direction and of Lecoq's politics:

> That's one of the attractive things about him. . . . He did not want to do Brecht, but he was very interested in discovering the popular roots of theatre. . . . So his whole practice was about giving voice to the people, giving expression to the people. His four main dramatic territories were all in their own way 'popular' art forms. It's not by chance that one of these was melodrama – the popular art form par excellence. He was interested in those basic situations of people saying goodbye, people in need. He reckoned that was his political statement.
>
> (Bradby 2002a)

It is fruitful to compare this disposition to the austerity and asceticism with which Decroux – also on the political 'left' – approached his own teaching and performance work. Although Marcel Marceau learned the technical grammar of mime from Decroux, his teacher was later to disavow the technically accomplished but 'popular mime' with which Marceau was to tour the world for over four decades.

Towards the end of this immediate post-war period, before he moved to Italy in 1948, Lecoq was invited to join *Les Comédiens de Grenoble* in Grenoble by its director, Jean Dasté, son-in-law of Jacques Copeau. Here, again, the interrelatedness between strands of practice within European modernism is evidenced when we learn that Dasté had also worked with Antonin Artaud some fifteen years earlier. It was Artaud, as Alison Hodge notes in her introduction to a book of essays on actor training, who 'called for a theatre which celebrated the non-verbal elements of consciousness . . . for a more sensuous physical actor . . . an "athlete of the heart"' (Hodge 2000: 6).

In the same period, through his exposure to Dasté, and **Léon Chancerel** (1886–1965), Lecoq first began to work with masks and explore the *commedia dell'arte*. Reflecting on this time, when he also worked with poet and writer, **Gabriel Cousin** (1918–), many of whose plays he was later to direct, Lecoq again emphasises the sporting connection: 'as we were athletes . . . our fundamental gestural language was based on the sports we practised: I was a swimmer, he was a runner. Sports, movement and theatre were already closely related' (Lecoq 2000: 4).

Commedia dell'arte is a theatrical tradition that dates back to sixteenth-century Italy and has its deep roots in the theatre of ancient Greece. *Commedia* has had a significant influence upon comic theatre throughout Europe ever since. Formally, *commedia* was improvised around a tight structure of stock characters (e.g. Pantalone and Harlequin), most of whom were masked, and incorporated various theatrical disciplines, including acrobatics, mime and slapstick. The challenge for twentieth-century theatre practitioners interested in *commedia*, such as Lecoq, has been how to invest it with more than merely a historical or archival significance.

During these three years in Grenoble and Paris we must register Lecoq's exposure to, and burgeoning interest in, various theatre forms that were to become central to his pedagogy and research, first in Italy and then from 1956 at the Paris school. Working with masks, *commedia dell'arte*, the nature of movement and a political and emotional commitment to 'popular' theatre forms all continued to inform his thinking, and remained – with varying degrees of emphasis – central features of the curriculum at the Paris school.

In 1948, Lecoq was invited to Italy to teach movement skills at the University of Padua, and so began an eight-year period during which time his reputation as a teacher, director and thinker blossomed. In Padua he began to direct plays at the University Theatre and here 'he claims to have discovered *le jeu de la Commedia Dell'Arte* in the markets of the town' (Frost and Yarrow 1990: 61). As we shall see, the idea of '*le jeu*', which at its simplest means 'play', lies at the very heart of Lecoq's analysis of acting. The various shades of meaning attached to '*le jeu*' will be examined in greater detail when Lecoq's own writing is considered in the second chapter of this book.

In Padua, Lecoq met a young sculptor and mask-maker called Amleto Sartori (Figure 1.1) and embarked on a partnership of great significance for his subsequent research and teaching: 'the masks made by Amleto and his son Donato still make up an integral part of my pedagogic tools today' (Lecoq 1987: 109). Amleto's concept of the neutral mask was a product of detailed discussion with Lecoq, and was initially constructed and modelled around the contours of Lecoq's own face. When Lecoq finally left Italy for Paris in 1956, Amleto Sartori presented him with a full set of leather *commedia* masks, which he continued to use until his death in 1999. Sartori adapted the techniques of Renaissance bookbinding to the task of fabricating leather *commedia* masks, and together for nearly a decade they researched and investigated the relationship between the form and theatrical function of the mask. While this 'great friendship' ended with Sartori's early death at the age of 46 in 1958, his son Donato continued to supply a range of masks for the school. A comment made by Lecoq many years later gives an indication that he had already seen the potential for political subversion in the 'Italian comedy':

> I don't bury myself in historical references. I try to rediscover the spirit of these forms. *Commedia* has nothing to do with those little Italian troupes who export

Figure 1.1 Jacques Lecoq with Amleto Sartori (1959)

precious entertainments. It's about misery, a world where life's a luxury. . . .
If you are thinking of *Commedia* forget about Italy.

(Hiley 1998: 40)

In 1951, Lecoq moved to Milan to join Paulo Grassi (1919–81) and
Giorgio Strehler (1921–97) at the Piccolo Theatre (Figure 1.2). Grassi,
an actor-director, and Strehler, a director, had founded the Piccolo in
1947 on an explicit anti-fascist ideology and with a commitment to
reaching working-class audiences. By the time Lecoq arrived, the partnership had already launched the *teatro stabile* movement that – by the
1960s – had established a network of permanent troupes throughout Italy. By 1951, however, the Piccolo already had a reputation
as one of Italy's leading theatres, and Strehler and Grassi invited the
young Lecoq to open a school there committed to the pedagogy of
movement. Shortly after arriving at the Piccolo, Lecoq introduced
Sartori to Strehler and all three worked together on his famous masked
production of Goldoni's *A Servant of Two Masters*. Lecoq collaborated
with Grassi and Strehler until 1956 and, during this time, worked on
over sixty productions, not only at the Piccolo, but for *teatro stabile*

theatres in Rome, Syracuse and Venice as well. He directed and choreographed in a wide range of theatrical styles, but was particularly engrossed by Greek tragedy, pantomime and *commedia*. In her chapter on Lecoq in *Apostles of Silence*, Myra Felner observes that:

> He continued the exploration of the Commedia he had begun with Dasté. He examined the ancient mime traditions – the Greek chorus, the acrobatic Roman mime. He was searching for the roots of movement in the theatre.
>
> (Felner 1985: 147)

It was during this period in Milan that Lecoq first met and worked with Dario Fo (1926–) (Figure 1.3). Both became members of a troupe committed to experimentation within a framework of popular theatre. In 1952 they created a couple of satirical and political reviews. These marked a major departure from the traditional 'safe' reviews which had until then been dominated by famous actors. Nearly fifty years

Figure 1.2 Piccolo Theatre, Milan, with Durano, Lecoq, Parenti, Carpi and Fo (1954)

later Fo received the Nobel Prize for Literature after a working life of writing, directing and performing theatre which had been resolutely anti-establishment – the Catholic Church, the State, the corruption of the ruling classes and the debilitating power of capitalism have all been the butt of his writing and theatre-making. Lecoq's and Fo's friendship and mutual respect continued until Lecoq's death in 1999. Here, recorded for a French television profile of Lecoq shortly before his death, the two men reflected on their early work together, and on the cultural and social conditions of Italy in the early 1950s:

DF: We were children back then.
     I was 23 and you were 25.
     So we were really just kids.

JL: We had no idea of the results of what we were doing.
     We just did it; we just made it up, but we had no idea.
     We weren't diplomats or strategic about anything.

DF: But there was a very important phenomenon that we were going through at the time.
     We were living among extraordinary renewal.
     We had to throw away everything and construct a world.
     The world had to be made all over again.

JL: There were no more rules.
     There were no more rules.
     We had to make up the game again – find new rules.

(Roy and Carasso 1999)

This snatch of dialogue between two old men of European theatre has a resonance and poignancy to it, not least because the conversation was recorded within a year of Lecoq's death. More importantly, perhaps, it reveals a strong feeling of optimism following the defeat of Fascism, and a sense that artists could – and should – empower themselves to invent afresh the rules of their particular creative work. For both these men the post-war landscape of Western theatre had to be re-mapped with different conventions and methods. In any attempt to understand what drove Lecoq it is essential to imagine the times and circumstances of his life as a child and young man. The collective and individual trauma of living through the Second World War, which so obviously shaped the perceptions of those who experienced it, was often matched

Figure 1.3 Dario Fo and Jacques Lecoq (1973)

by an overwhelming sense of the need for cultural, social and political renewal when the war had ended. It is always important to place the subsequent working lives of both Lecoq and Fo within this historical and cultural context.

In 1956, at the age of thirty-five, Lecoq returned to France and established the school he was to direct until his death in 1999. Much of the rest of this book concerns itself with an examination of what he was trying to achieve in Paris's tenth arrondissement at 57 rue du Faubourg St Denis. While it is clear that the school was never simply a vehicle to *train* actors with the skills that Lecoq himself had acquired when working with Dasté in Grenoble, and later during his time in Italy, these years were crucial in constructing a platform upon which to launch the research and teaching that followed. As we noted earlier, most of the great figures of twentieth-century theatre who were committed to rethinking the nature and direction of acting used the rehearsal studio as their arena for testing ideas and hypotheses. For Lecoq – at least from 1956 – the school was his 'laboratory' and students – rather than professional actors – were the subjects of his experiments. Clearly, his time in Italy was an episode of intense and energetic exploration of dramatic form, and a period that firmly established the theatrical territory he was to inhabit for the rest of his life. Lecoq's relationship in Italy with figures such as Strehler, Sartori and Fo, and his immersion in mask work, Greek chorus, improvisation, movement and the politics of popular theatre, all provided the framework and context which were to provoke the questions he continued to pose – of both himself and his students – for the next forty years from his base in Paris.

THE PARIS SCHOOLS (1956–99)

In life I want students to be alive, and on stage I want them to be artists.

(Translated from *Le Corps Poétique* for obituaries
in *Total Theatre*: Berkoff *et al.* (1999))

I am nobody; I am only a neutral point through which you must pass in order to better articulate your own theatrical voice. I am only there to place obstacles in your path so you can find your own way around them

(Lecoq in conversation with Simon McBurney:
McBurney (1991a))

The school moves; otherwise it dies.

(Lecoq 1987: 120)

From 1956, Lecoq devoted himself to running a school of:

Mime and Theatre based on movement and the human body . . . a school of dramatic creation; it relies on knowledge of the organic and emotional dynamics of man and nature . . . the school concerns itself with theatre to be created; this theatre belongs to the pupils, their ideas, their quest.

(Brochure advertising the school in the 1980s)

During its first twenty years, the school seemed always to be on the move within Paris, apparently shifting from one less than satisfactory space to another. Lecoq records the difficult conditions in which sometimes they had to function. For example, in the early 1970s the school was based in the American Centre on the Boulevard Raspail, and Lecoq notes wryly that it was a 'vast, unheated space in which we worked on lessons wrapped in blankets' (Lecoq 2000: 12). Despite the unsatisfactory nature of such a nomadic existence, the experience helped Lecoq to formulate his thoughts on the relationship between space, movement and creative discovery: ideas that were later to be explored more formally with the introduction of LEM (Laboratoire d'Étude du Mouvement). Different spaces proposed different possibilities for creative work and Lecoq was happy to be provoked by these:

> There were experiments with 'danse concrète' which ran parallel to 'musique concrète'. It was also in this period that I tried to create theatre using the rules of sport. Two teams performed around the same theme – jealousy, for example, within the parameters of a basketball court ... this was 'theatre ball'. And it was also towards the end of this roaming around, at the Centre Américain, that the school discovered other artistic areas: melodrama, the storyteller mime, comic strips and tribunes.
>
> (Lecoq 1987: 118)

Finally, in 1976, he found the premises (Le Central) 'that seemed destined for us' (Lecoq 2000: 12) at 57 rue du Faubourg St Denis in Paris's tenth arrondissement. Most appropriately, given Lecoq's early and abiding interest in sport, Le Central had been a gymnasium devoted to boxing (Figure 1.4). It had not only witnessed some of the great boxing contests of the first half of the twentieth century, it was near to Copeau's birthplace and where **Louis Jouvet** (1887–1951) lived and worked. Moreover, Le Central had inspired Marcel Carné's film, *Air de Paris*. When they took over the building it was, according to his wife Fay, almost a complete ruin and without electricity, changing rooms and toilets. Today, the 'ruin' has all the necessary facilities, the foyer and passageways decorated with photographs, posters and notices, and, at the heart of the building, a massive hall – once a boxing gymnasium – encircled high up by a precarious-looking wooden balcony. A lot of wood. Here, you can almost smell its history and feel the presence of the sporting figures who once gave life to this extraordinary space, 'redolent of that 1930's world of the *Popular Front* which was so well captured by **Jean Renoir** [1894–1979] in his films' (Bradby 2002a).

Characteristically, the school does not shout its presence to the world outside: only a small nondescript plaque on a heavy steel security door leading on to the street suggests that down a long narrow

Figure 1.4
Le Central
Sporting
Club (1954)

courtyard lies the building which Lecoq, with his wife, Fay, has turned into one of Europe's leading laboratories of contemporary theatre practice. Rue du Faubourg St Denis itself is a busy, raucous and noisy thoroughfare. Today, much of it seems more or less equally devoted to the selling of sex, fruit, vegetables, fast food and cheap electrical gadgets. Training actors to move at number 57 sits happily alongside a variety of other uses to which the human body may be employed – a good place for a school devoted to exploring *nature* as well as *culture*; the perfect location to explore the 'le jeu de bouffons'; and, perhaps, the best possible site to enjoy the heightened emotions of melodrama, or the plebeian camaraderie of the Greek chorus. Far better here than in the more refined bourgeois *quartiers* of the seventh and eighth arrondissements.

The short extract from a brochure – quoted on p. 16 – hints at the essence of what Lecoq's school was trying to explore: the philosophical assumptions which remained more or less constant over forty-three years, and which underpinned all the practical teaching strategies employed by Lecoq and his colleagues. A school engaged with 'dramatic creation' rather than merely realising the theatrical edicts of other 'masters'. A school that would spend time investigating the 'emotional dynamics' of – and between – man and nature. A school concerned with 'theatre *to be* created'. Observe here a forward-looking stance that aspires to construct a theatre of the future, not simply *re-presenting* the theatre that is already known. Perhaps, above all, a school which – without any apparent awkwardness – speaks of '*mime* and theatre based on movement and the human body' (brochure advertising the school).

While Lecoq himself led the school, a small team of other tutors with particular skills and specialisms worked alongside him. Most tutors have been students at the school and should also have attended the third – optional – year in pedagogy. His second wife – Scottish-born Fay – led a team of administrators and often dealt with the world outside the school on behalf of her husband. Fay regularly toured with Lecoq when he was conducting workshops, or offering his lecture-demonstration – *Tout bouge* – in different countries of the world. Where English translation was required, Fay would provide it. Entry to the school's two-year course is upon the presentation of a satisfactory curriculum vitae and teacher's reference, which should testify to the applicant's movement and acting ability – or at least potential. No further audition or test of skill and potential is required at this point. Typically, about 100 students – 'more than 50 nations have been represented' (extract from school brochure in the mid-1980s) – enter the school every September. Although the first term is officially a trial period during which both school and pupils decide whether the relationship will work, rarely more than ten students leave at this juncture, and when they do it is largely of their own volition. The end of the first year, however, is a very different matter. At this point, Lecoq and his team would select those who were deemed suitable to progress into the second year. Sometimes as many as forty or fifty might have been asked to go at this point, leaving a core group of about thirty-five or forty.

Successful passage into the second year has never been predicated upon any formal examination or assessment and was based on Lecoq's sense of who was 'open' (*disponible*) enough to benefit from a further year at the school. While it is stressed that those leaving the school are not being judged on the basis of their acting skills, it is hard to imagine that most departing students exit with much sense of pleasure and achievement. For first-year students it is a time of great tension as they await the verdicts of their tutors. Nonetheless, the school is anxious to stress that the decision to ask students to leave is not about perceptions of quality, success or failure. Thomas Prattki, who took over as Director of Pedagogy at the school after Lecoq's death in 1999, puts it like this:

> Maybe the student's vision is already clear . . . they no longer need the school. It's not a judgement about the quality of the student. Sometimes they confuse a desire for life with a desire for theatre. It's not about whether a student 'fits into the Lecoq approach'.

> (Prattki 2001)

In addition to a third and entirely optional year on pedagogy, from 1977 Lecoq launched LEM (translated as Laboratory for the Study of Movement) as an evening class for those interested in studying the relationship between the human body and the constructed space in which it moves. In a brochure Lecoq described LEM as 'a laboratory devoted to research . . . a place of experiment and of science' (author's translation). While LEM was not concerned with theatrical creation as such, the course focused on understanding the dramatic potential of objects and materials and the spatial relationships between them. Elsewhere in the same brochure Lecoq writes that the course studies 'the dynamic of colours, their movement, their texture, their speed . . . and their relationship with the body and human passions' (author's translation). From such descriptions we can detect both a poetic and abstract quality to these enquiries, although for students attending LEM the actual process is a largely practical one entailing a considerable amount of *making*. One task was to construct balsa wood models that sought to capture and express the dynamic of the relationship between particular objects in space. As the word 'laboratory' implies, Lecoq conducted these workshops very much in a spirit of research and open-ended enquiry. He led the course jointly with an architect, and one imagines that the experience provided an opportunity for him to test and play with ideas – a freedom which was perhaps less available within the structure of the two-year course. Today, LEM continues to be a popular and significant adjunct to the main business of the school. It is examined in more detail in the next chapter of the book.

From 1956 until his death in 1999, Lecoq directed most of his considerable energy and imagination into the school. However, throughout this period – and certainly during the first fifteen to twenty years of the school's life – Lecoq used non-teaching time to engage in various directing and movement choreography projects. Fay Lecoq records that, from the late 1950s he was movement director for a BBC production of Prokofiev's *Peter and the Wolf*, worked with the opera in Rome, directed Mayakovsky's *The Flea* in Berlin, choreographed for Les Ballets Contemporains in Lille, and regularly produced and choreographed Greek tragedies at Syracuse in Sicily (Figure 1.5). For the latter, according to Fay Lecoq, he would take his actors from Paris and rehearse for several weeks in Rome before opening the productions in Syracuse. In addition, the school's publicity announces that he collaborated with the Comédie Française and the Schiller Theatre and advised on various French television productions. We know, too, that Lecoq was happy to offer dramaturgical advice and support to ex-students whose companies he much admired, such as Mummenschanz, Footsbarn and Théâtre de Complicité.

From the 1980s, as the school became well established, consolidated its international reputation and significantly increased its student intake,

Figure 1.5
Travel
Journals:
Company
Lecoq (1959)

Lecoq had less and less time to devote to directing and choreographic projects. However, the annual summer school in Paris continued, as did a master class that was only offered every four years. The latter allowed Lecoq to communicate and share special discoveries made from his research during the intervening period. The first of these was in 1964 and included Steven Berkoff as one of its participants. Alongside these regular commitments, he would also accept – but increasingly selectively – invitations to run classes and workshops in different parts of the world. For example, in 1982, at the request of the Arts Council of Great Britain, he ran the two-week British Summer School of Mime in London. In 1988 he conducted a five-day workshop and performed *Tout bouge* (*Everything Moves*) – his seminal lecture-demonstration – at London's Queen Elizabeth Hall for the International Workshop Festival (IWF) (Figure 1.6). By the time of his death, Lecoq had performed *Tout bouge* on numerous occasions across the world, and particularly in Japan, China, Australia and North America. In August 1990, at the invitation of Dick McCaw, who was now running the IWF, he taught a LEM masterclass with Krikor Belekian and his daughter, Pascale – both architects – at the Royal Scottish Academy of Music and Drama in Glasgow. The workshop examined relationships between movement of the body, theatre and architecture, and was attended by architects and visual artists as well as theatre practitioners.

At the time of writing – three years after his death – the school that Lecoq meticulously constructed continues to accept students. Fay Lecoq maintains overall administrative and managerial leadership, working with a college of teachers. From October 1999 until he left in July 2002, Director of Pedagogy at the school was Thomas Prattki, who had begun teaching there in 1993. Immediately after Lecoq's death, there was considerable speculation as to whether the institution could survive without him – whether, indeed, it could attract pupils without the appeal of his intellectual leadership and provocation. However, the school recruits as healthily as ever, thus offering an interesting comparison with other similar establishments where the death of the 'master' – of the 'guru' – would certainly have precipitated closure. Fay Lecoq remains committed to overseeing its development for as long as she is able, but clearly the school will continue to change and experiment – perhaps in ways unimagined by its founder.

Figure 1.6 Jacques Lecoq: *Tout bouge* (1990)

JACQUES LECOQ AND THE WESTERN TRADITION OF ACTOR TRAINING

TRAINING ACTORS

> (Actor training) is arguably the most important development in modern Western theatre making. Actor training in Europe and North America is a phenomenon of the twentieth century, and has come to inform both the concept and construction of the actor's role, and consequently the entire dramatic process.
>
> (Hodge 2000: 1)

We have so far traced the main contours of Lecoq's life and considered in some detail his school and its development in Paris. Earlier, I argued that Lecoq's assiduous, but unfinished research into the pedagogy of actor training that privileged the performer's body located him within a wider cultural and historical tradition – a tradition that regularly offered a challenge to existing notions of the business of acting and, by implication, the nature of theatre itself.

Alison Hodge suggests in the introduction to her book of essays (2000) that the development and formalisation of actor training in the West has been largely a twentieth-century phenomenon. While the systematic training of actors in Eastern forms of dance and drama such as Kathakali from Southern India and Noh theatre from Japan dates back to the Middle Ages, in the West – although we can identify some elaborate traditions and rituals of actor apprenticeship and 'learning on the job' – the first specialist European drama school, Le Conservatoire National d'Art Dramatique in Paris, was not established until 1786. Indeed, while in the nineteenth century a small number of conservatoires were opened in a few major European cities, it is not until the twentieth century that any significant expansion in formal actor training began to take hold.

The systematic organisation of the training of actors in the West has an interesting and symbiotic relationship to a number of other distinguishing features of twentieth-century European and North American theatre: its increasing commercialisation and commodification, the rise of the professional theatre director, the influence of 'scientific' research and psychology on the performing arts, and a growing interest in – and sometimes an extreme romanticisation of – Eastern dramatic forms and their associated training regimes. In this sense, training for the theatre reflects the development of mass education in the West, and is both cause and consequence of industrialising societies' need for a partially educated workforce. Training and education are not gifted by benign authorities, but are both fought for by different constituencies at particular times, *and* are the necessary corollary of industrialisation and market forces.

At least in one sense Lecoq is no different from other key innovators in twentieth-century actor training – for example, Stanislavsky, Meyerhold, Copeau, Brecht, Decroux and Grotowski. What all these figures share are wider territories of intellectual interest, which spread well beyond the narrow inculcation of 'technical' skills. It is impossible to understand different models of actor training without considering the kind of theatre or performance such pedagogies were designed to address. None of these men sought simply to equip young actors for the theatrical *status quo*. In often sharply contrasting ways, each was trying to shift and redefine the parameters and possibilities of what constituted theatre and what its purpose should be. If the rationale for these models of actor training had been simply to help the student actor deliver text more persuasively, or move with greater fluidity and effectiveness on stage – all in the service of a naturalistic or realistic theatre – then our interest might be equally limited.

The models of actor training practised and theorised by those figures identified above have all proposed relatively different answers to a similar set of questions – Lecoq no less than Meyerhold or Stanislavsky. Questions such as these:

- What kinds of relationship are possible between performers and spectators?
- Where do the boundaries between theatre and other art forms or cultural practices begin and end?
- What sorts of metaphors are useful to express the essence of this particular approach to training?
- What is the relationship between the actor's body and the actor's mind, and, indeed, is it helpful to pose these two as separate entities, the former 'directing', or controlling, the latter?
- How does the model of training understand the body and its construction?

- Is the attempt to define and create a *universal* language of theatre either possible or desirable?
- How does the training regime acknowledge, deal with and utilise (for performance) notions of the 'conscious' and 'unconscious' mind?
- To what extent does the idea of, and quest for 'presence', have any validity in a programme of actor training?
- How far does the training model seek to engage with issues and ideas beyond performance and theatre?

Any attempt to understand how different models of actor training actually work demands that the philosophical and cultural assumptions which inform practical teaching methods are teased out and identified. While these questions may appear to be of little interest beyond the academy, answers to these enquiries have a concrete and tangible bearing on performance dramaturgy, such as the efficacy of particular approaches to acting, the spectator's ability to 'read' the signs of performance, and the ideological inflections and nuances of any piece of theatre and its component elements. The intelligent and creative director or actor has little choice but to have some kind of informed grasp of these issues. Teacher and director, Philip Zarrilli, neatly summarises the argument as follows:

> Every time an actor performs, he or she implicitly enacts a 'theory' of acting – a set of assumptions about the conventions and style which guide his or her performance, the structure of actions which he or she performs, the shape that those actions take . . . and the relationship to the audience. Informing these assumptions are culture-specific assumptions about the body–mind relationship, the nature of the self, the emotions/feelings, and performance context.
>
> (1995: 4)

When interrogating the work of any radical and visionary teacher such as Lecoq, there is a delicate balance to be struck between locating their practice in a wider cultural-historical context on the one hand, and grasping the extent to which their work and ideas represent genuinely new and innovatory formulations and propositions on the other. To err too much on the side of the former is to run the risk of becoming overly derivative, or determinist in explaining a particular individual's contribution to their art form. However, to overemphasise notions of originality, or, indeed – at its most extreme – of 'genius', is to idealise artistic process, and to uproot that figure from both history and the contemporary culture in which he or she practised.

In addition, there are two other – related – problems: how to define what we mean by the term 'influence'; and how to use the luxurious commodity of hindsight with intelligence and sensitivity. The issue about *influence* seems to pivot around how consciously and manifestly one subject acknowledges that his or her practice draws upon and develops ideas from another. The problem with hindsight is that its lofty vantage point encourages the commentator to make connections and to identify *influences* that were never explicit or realised by the subject at the time he or she was a practising artist. Thus, while Lecoq acknowledged both Artaud and Copeau as significant in shaping his own thinking, the linkages one might want to make with, for example, Brecht and Meyerhold are more difficult to uncover and tease out. Similarities, connections, discontinuities and overlaps are there to be unearthed, but with Lecoq this is especially difficult, since he offers few clues in his writing as to which other historical figures he either admired, or for whom he had little time.

COPEAU AND ARTAUD: A COMPLEX LEGACY

Copeau's legacy for French and certain strands of European theatre has been well documented. His missionary vision for the rebirth of French theatre and training methods rooted in movement and corporeality have greatly influenced subsequent generations of French theatre-makers. Schematically, these can be divided into two – overlapping – groups. On the one hand, there were those such as Charles Dullin, Louis Jouvet, Jean Dasté and Michel Saint-Denis, who worked largely in text-based, popular and often politically committed theatre during the inter- and post-war years; and on the other, a select group of individuals dedicated to the reinvention and modernisation of mime: Étienne Decroux, Jean-Louis Barrault, Jacques Lecoq and Marcel Marceau. While the work of Decroux and Marceau stands as a monument to the project of establishing mime as an autonomous art form distinct from dance and theatre, Barrault and Lecoq chose to inhabit a more expansive territory in which mime was redefined and had a significant, but only partial stake. In fact, Lecoq straddles both these groupings, as his early post-war theatre work was with Jean Dasté, and it is the latter who provides the most tangible link to Copeau.

Lecoq joined Dasté's Compagnie de Comédiens in Grenoble shortly after the war and stayed with him until the ensemble moved to St Étienne in 1947. Dasté – Copeau's son-in-law – had been invited to Grenoble by former members of the cultural wing of the Resistance, and his purpose was nothing less than the reinvention of popular theatre: 'to discover folly, festivity, the fundamental freedom of being' (Dasté 1977: 43). In *The Moving Body*, Lecoq remarks that 'through Dasté I discovered masked performance and Japanese Noh theatre, both of which have had a powerful influence on me' (2000: 5). Another link to Copeau was through Claude Martin, with whom Lecoq worked on improvisation during the immediate post-war period. Martin had been a pupil of Dullin, who too had trained with Copeau at Le Vieux Columbier.

The main emphasis at Copeau's school, Le Vieux Columbier, and later when he moved his company to Burgundy, was on movement preparation for the actor and on play. Certainly, Lecoq shares with Copeau a belief that movement training for the actor should not primarily be directed towards fitness, athleticism or technique, but must be harnessed as a means towards spontaneity, playfulness and creativity. In addition, physical training was crucial in the process of generating the chemistry of *ensemble*. Significantly, and in line with many avant-garde artists of the time, Copeau's philosophy was also predicated upon a wider belief that in contemporary industrial society the modern 'body' was atrophied and dulled of its sensations. Christopher Innes in *Avant Garde Theatre* (1993) characterises the key quality of this cultural movement as 'primitivism' or, in other words, the desire to return to an imagined state of simplicity. This romantic yearning for a purer more *wholesome* existence echoes the philosopher, **Jean-Jacques Rousseau**'s (1712–78) ideal of the 'noble savage': someone uncorrupted by the debilitating complexities and demands of modern industrial and *bourgeois* society.

After rejecting **Émile Jaques-Dalcroze**'s (1865–1950) system of *eurhythmics* on the basis that it led to a narcissistic approach to the body, by 1921 Copeau had wholeheartedly embraced **Georges Hébert**'s (1875–1957) method of 'natural gymnastics'. Hébert was an influential theorist who had revolutionised approaches to physical education in Europe during the first few decades of the century. According to

Hébert, a key feature of man's corporeal alienation in industrialised societies was that, as we grow into adulthood, our muscular development becomes limited, constrained and deformed. As a consequence we lose the instinct for play, and hence our expressivity and ability to be creative. Thus, for Copeau, an essential task in the training of the creative actor was to rediscover the child's instinct for play. Essentially, this was to be achieved not through accretion and the addition of skills and techniques, but through a process of 'shedding' and stripping away, thereby removing those socialised impediments to spontaneous play. John Rudlin, in his essay on Copeau for the Hodge compilation, notes the link between Hébert's and Lecoq's teaching:

> Jacques Lecoq used the Hébert method in his school in Paris: 'pull, push, climb, walk, run, jump, lift, carry, attack, defend, swim. These actions trace a physical circuitry in sensitive bodies in which emotions are imprinted.' Lecoq himself came from a sporting background, and his is perhaps a larger claim for the potential of the method than Copeau would have believed possible.
>
> (Rudlin in Hodge 2000: 68)

It is impossible to underestimate the significance of the insight that movement can nurture the capacity for play for generations of – selected – theatre-makers and trainers from Copeau's time to the present. It is certainly a most important dimension of Lecoq's pedagogy and practice at the Paris school. However, the extent to which Lecoq also shares this 'primitivism' and distaste for the 'modern' with early twentieth-century members of the cultural avant-garde such as Copeau, Artaud and Hébert is open to debate. It is an issue that will be considered more closely in the next chapter when examining his writing. For some commentators, Lecoq's use of the neutral mask and his preoccupation with the apparently uncluttered innocence of childhood is misconceived and philosophically dubious territory. On the other hand, the lengths to which Lecoq goes to circumscribe and contextualise the use of, for example, the neutral mask suggest that – on this score – he self-consciously distances himself from those avant-garde *primitivists* within the modernist movement.

Beyond the centrality of movement and play to both Copeau and Lecoq's pedagogies, the other main territories of shared interest lay in mask work, *commedia dell'arte* and Greek tragedy. Copeau introduced mask work in the early days of Le Vieux Columbier, but it rapidly became a critical element of his teaching. Instead of Lecoq's *neutral* mask he employed the term 'noble', after the expressionless masks worn by the aristocracy until the eighteenth century in an attempt to remain anonymous. Working with these masks became central to his major project of achieving simplicity and neutrality in his students. In this condition they could find a fresh and intuitive relationship with objects, and execute actions which, Copeau argued, articulated the authenticity he sought in acting. The mask as a training tool had the potential of representing 'the quintessence of theatrical transformation and provided the key to the actor's approach to the role' (Felner 1985: 42).

When comparing the goals, strategies and techniques of both Copeau and Lecoq, it is tempting to overstress the common features of their work. Both identified movement and play as a central conceptual and practical element to their teaching; both focused on the mask, the chorus and the *commedia dell'arte* as instruments for educating the *modern* actor, and – in the case of Greek tragedy and the 'Italian Comedy' – as a vehicle for theatrical innovation and renewal. Both, too, were committed to wider educational goals beyond a narrow and vocational training, believing that one could not make effective and creative actors without also educating them 'for life'. Both, in other words, seem to share a common humanism that extends well beyond the stage itself.

However, it is a great oversimplification to reduce Lecoq's work to a late twentieth-century version of Copeau's. In one crucial way, at least, there is a significant difference between the two men and their vision of training for theatre. While Copeau was certainly a radical in the sense that he almost single-handedly introduced the notion of an in-depth and continuous training for young actors at a time when French theatre was artistically and culturally bankrupt, the progressive innovations in pedagogy he offered in his schools were designed to return theatre to the classics. Unlike Lecoq, his experiments in training were not directed towards a 'new' theatre. Essentially, Copeau was trying to discover fresh ways to do justice to the traditional repertoire of European theatre. By 'purifying' French theatre of its tricks and by shedding it of *cabotinage* – the phoney gimmicks of nineteenth-century performance – Copeau believed he was preparing theatre for a return to its imagined past. Thus, although Copeau remained one of Lecoq's main 'reference points', there were, nonetheless, significant differences between their practice, overall aspirations and objectives.

In an interview with Jean Perret in *Le Théâtre du geste* Lecoq acknowledges the influence of Copeau in the early stages of his career: 'it's true that the proximity of Jacques Copeau and the *Copiaux* affected me and had a direct influence' (Lecoq 1987: 109). However, a little later in the same interview, when asked whether he was more influenced by Copeau or Artaud and Dullin, Lecoq replies 'much more by Artaud and Dullin' (1987: 109). Thus, by the time of this interview – 1986/7 – it seems that it is the spirit of Artaud rather than Copeau which resonates most strongly. Clearly Lecoq and Artaud share a commitment to a dynamic visual theatre where movement and physicality are the primary motors of dramatic expression. Inevitably, perhaps, Artaud also connects with Copeau through Louis Jouvet who had set up his own school after a year at Le Vieux Columbier. Artaud attended Jouvet's school and spoke passionately of the experience:

> We act with our deepest hearts, we act with our hands, our feet, all our muscles, and all our limbs. We feel the object, we smell it, we handle it, see it, hear it . . . all to find there is nothing there, no accessories.
>
> (cited in Bradby 1984: 5)

In this comment we can find echoes of Lecoq's own commitment to acting as primarily a corporeal and physical project, and to neutral mask exercises in which students are invited to experience the material world in 'a state of receptiveness to everything around us, with no inner conflict' (Lecoq 2000: 36). What perhaps is more surprising – given his reputation as a wild and visionary seer – is that, for a period of his life, Artaud worked on a disciplined and rigorous physical training scheme for actors, believing, like Lecoq, that his vision of theatre could only be realised by performers with sharp movement skills and sensitivities. Where, one imagines, Lecoq might have had reservations about Artaud's ideas is with the latter's mission to rediscover the primitive ritual function of theatre. Artaud's absolute rejection of logic and reason and – in their place – his advocacy of irrational spontaneity, delirium and the generation of trance-like states among actors and spectators alike contrasts strongly with Lecoq's suspicion of the overly mystical or therapeutic aspects of theatre. The use of trance and delirium do not figure in an inventory of teaching techniques employed at Lecoq's school!

It would be possible to devote considerably more space to teasing out connections between Lecoq's ideas and those of other major thinkers and practitioners of twentieth-century theatre. However, the danger in such a project is that it becomes a purely academic exercise that loses touch with the reality of how Lecoq actually worked, both as pedagogue and researcher. The argument forcibly put to me by a number of the people interviewed for this book was that, while Lecoq was, of course, very aware of particular historical traditions of theatre practice – the dramatic territories of tragedy, *commedia* and melodrama, for example – the pulsating heart of all his work was the human body and its movement in space. David Bradby makes this point very clearly:

> He was not primarily interested in making connections with historical figures. He was really interested in the body and how it moved, and that was the centre of everything. To ask if he was more influenced by Copeau or Artaud, or whoever, is missing the point: missing the centre of his own natural passion and the way he developed his own teaching.
>
> (Bradby 2002a)

JACQUES LECOQ: THE BODY AND CULTURE

This first chapter of the book attempts to do two main things:

1   to trace the contours and details of Lecoq's working life; and
2   to look briefly at the bigger historical and cultural picture that frames this particular life.

The assumption here is that to attend to the wider context of a body of work helps to bring focus and perspective upon that work itself. Having identified a relationship with the practice of two of Lecoq's historical forebears – Copeau and Artaud – this section is concluded by briefly investigating two contemporary phenomena, an understanding of which helps to provide context to Lecoq's life and work. Lecoq's school has thrived at a time when we can observe two features of Western culture: one concerns the increasing production of – and demand for – theatre which has a strong visual dimension and where the actors' bodies deliberately signify as much as words spoken; the other connects to wider preoccupations with the body in both intellectual enquiry and in many aspects of popular culture.

PHYSICAL AND OTHER THEATRES

At the beginning of this account I noted that Lecoq was a central figure in a loose movement of theatre artists, academics and teachers who, towards the end of the twentieth century, proposed – through theory and practice – that it is the performer's *live* body more than the spoken text which gives theatre its defining identity in an age dominated culturally by film, television and digital media. To put it another way, it is the body and its movement through and in space that is the crucial generator of meaning and significance in contemporary theatre. Performance work that foregrounds these features seems to have drawn its influence from dance, theatre and the visual arts. Indeed, one of its important qualities is that it is work that apparently cares little for the traditional boundaries between different art forms.

Over the last two decades, much of this practice has come to be labelled 'physical theatre' or 'visual theatre'. By and large, the term is more of a marketing tool than a useful framework for analysing new developments in theatre practice. Lecoq himself gives little evidence in his writing of bothering with the term *physical theatre* – or its equivalents – preferring instead to reclaim mime from *pantomime* and the limitations of white-faced illusion. Although lacking analytical rigour, *physical theatre* is still a useful term to signpost a significant increase in performance work that privileges the actor's body rather than the spoken word. Ana Sanchez-Colberg offers a way of delineating this loose body of work:

> The term itself – 'physical theatre' – denotes a hybrid character and is testimony to its double legacy in both avant-garde theatre and dance. ... The locating of physical theatre within the avant-garde means that attention must be given to issues of anti-establishment within the context of alienation and transgression common to both forms. ... This body focus needs to be seen as arising from a progressive devaluation of language and a move towards a non-verbal idiom.
>
> (Sanchez-Colberg 1996: 40)

While Sanchez-Colberg's account is helpful in interrogating aspects of *physical theatre* as a cultural phenomenon, the picture she paints is a partial one. If we consider the range of theatrical forms which privilege the visual and movement dimensions of the language of performance, we discover a rather wider diversity of practice than she suggests. In addition to the legacies of modern dance and the theatrical avant-garde we should recognise other traditions that have also fed and shaped the contemporary phenomena of physical or movement theatres. To dance and the avant-garde we should add performance or live art, *popular theatre*, which includes circus, vaudeville and street performance, Eastern dance theatre and, of course, the French mime tradition. The conventions of the latter divide, in the two decades following the end of the Second World War, into the tightly codified movement 'grammar' of Étienne Decroux, and Lecoq's own physical preparation for a 'new theatre' or modern mime.

A superficial interpretation of this 'explosion' of *physical theatres* across Europe and North America since the early 1980s is to regard these simplistically as a direct expression – or outcome – of cultural formations which have increasingly demoted the value of the spoken word. Consequently – so the rhetoric goes – contemporary Western cultures seem to have downgraded the *literary*, and thus the cannon of great European playwriting has been usurped in favour of a visual, sensual and muscular form of new theatre. Seductive as such a reading might be to the aficionados of *physical theatre*, it is an unhistorical interpretation and inflates the supremacy of this mode of theatre production over more traditional writer-dominated forms. In his introduction to a recently published book of essays – *Jacques Lecoq and the British Theatre* – Franc Chamberlain reminds the reader that, notwithstanding the significance of Lecoq's teaching for contemporary Western theatre, and the rise of other forms of physical performance, *devised* theatre practice is still largely ignored and marginalised in most accounts of modern drama. Chamberlain's point is reinforced by the 2001 edition of *The New Penguin Dictionary of Theatre* which succeeds in omitting any reference to Lecoq at all.

Thus, the picture is inevitably more complex than a cursory glance might suggest. While since the early 1980s in Britain there has certainly been a significant increase in work that one might wish to label 'physical theatre', to suggest that before this period text-based *literary* theatre was monolithic in its domination is to ignore historical evidence. Although working from the play-text has been the overriding paradigm for British and – to a lesser extent – European theatre, other forms that challenge this hegemony have consistently intervened and nagged away throughout the twentieth century. Within the traditions of popular theatre, mime, performance art and the numerous, but sporadic, incursions of the avant-garde, the visual and physical languages of theatre have been in the ascendant.

In conclusion, although we are forced to note the increasing popularity of theatre forms that privilege movement and performer physicality, particularly in Britain, but also in Europe and North America, empirical evidence alone does not answer to the question of 'why such an increase at this historical juncture?' Lecoq, however, offers one kind of explanation:

> Mime becomes popular in a transitional period when theatre is in decline and is moving towards renewal. Theatre needs a heightened sense of movement because when the spoken word cannot express itself fully, it returns to the language of the body.

> (Vidal 1988)

Here, Lecoq is suggesting the presence of a cyclical pattern where, at certain historical junctures, 'speaking theatre' exhausts itself and can only be replenished by returning to the 'language of the body'. This kind of explanation has perhaps a particular appeal in Britain, where one is bound to note the weight on mainstream theatre practice – and on drama training – of a literary dramatic tradition going back at least to Shakespeare, Marlowe and Jonson. That an upsurge of *physical theatres* is particularly evident in the UK is sometimes explained as a long overdue reaction to the dominance of text based theatre – a much needed 'catching up' with the practices of continental Europe and beyond. The problem, however, remains of explaining why such a significant increase should occur at this particular historical moment. There is, too, a concern that all-embracing explanations which rest upon the notion of 'cycles' of cultural behaviour ignore the specifics of historical circumstances in different countries. Below, I consider another factor: the almost obsessive concern with the body in popular culture and as an object of scrutiny in a wide number of academic disciplines.

THE RISE – AND RISE – OF THE BODY IN CONTEMPORARY CULTURE

Often, developments in drama are analysed as if theatre as an art form stood outside – and independent of – society: a model that speaks of theatre *and* society rather than theatre *in* society. In fact, theatre – like any artistic practice – has an intimate, though complex, relationship with wider socio-historical, political and cultural circumstances. Maria Shevtsova, writing about the sociology of drama, likens theatre to a seismograph: 'it picks up tremors below the social surface, alerting audiences to dangers which may remain latent or actually erupt' (Shevtsova 1989: 184). Cultural theorist, Raymond Williams, argues that trends and movements in theatre cannot simply be explained by individual choices and decisions, but that they are also an expression of wider cultural shifts in feeling and thinking. The essence of Williams' *cultural materialist* analysis of theatre is neatly summarised by Stephen Regan:

> The methods or conventions of drama are not just technical preferences; they are, at the same time, ideas of reality and ways of seeing life that have been shaped by the interests and assumptions of a particular culture.
>
> (Regan 2000: 50)

So, in fact, theatre is not merely a 'seismograph picking up tremors . . .', but at the same time is actually *one* of those tremors. It follows, therefore, that if we are to try to understand why, for example, there has been a dramatic increase in forms of physical theatre in certain countries of the West over the last two decades, at least part of that account will take us into territories outside theatre itself. It is an inadequate explanation to suggest that the physical theatre phenomenon is simply the coincidental consequence of all the autonomous choices of performers and theatre-makers predisposed – for whatever reasons – to give pre-eminence to performers' physical and movement qualities.

What distinguishes this particular period is that – outside the arena of theatre and drama – the human body has become central to the enquiries of other disciplines, many apparently quite unconnected to theatre practice. Since the 1970s, the body has become pre-eminent in social thought, and often remorselessly examined in subjects such as sociology, economics, cultural studies, psychology, health studies and sports science. Beyond purely academic concerns, within the territory of 'popular culture', interest in personal health, beauty, diet, sexual attraction, fitness and ageing has reached near obsessive proportions. As early as 1970, cultural theorist Jean Baudrillard was observing that:

At the present time everything would seem to indicate that the body has become an object of salvation. It has literally replaced the soul in this moral and ideological function.

(cited in Featherstone *et al.* 1991: 393)

Why, then, this interest in the body? Broadly, there are two kinds of argument put forward to explain the trend. One concerns human identity, and the other capitalism's need to turn the body into a marketable *commodity* so that money – profits – can be made from it. In his introduction to *The Body and Social Theory* (1993) Chris Shilling argues that the pre-eminence of the body within contemporary thought and popular culture is rooted in the elusive quest to discover the nature of personal identity. Here, it is argued that, in contemporary Western societies, declining religious and political beliefs have encouraged people to look elsewhere for those meanings that help to define personal identity and selfhood. In these societies – variously described as 'late capitalist', 'post-industrial' or postmodern – it is the body in consumer culture which becomes the main bearer of symbolic value for our identity and, therefore, needs to be engaged in all manner of ways. Working on the body, dressing the body, decorating it, altering its shape, keeping it fit and in good health, disguising it or reinventing it where necessary – all these become activities for people concerned with defining and sustaining a sense of self and personal identity in late capitalist societies. If this hypothesis is even broadly correct, then a large variety of contemporary cultural activities – from keep-fit to fashion, from sports science to plastic surgery, from the club scene to physical theatre – can be given an overall explanatory context. The rise of various types of physical theatre, it might be argued, reflects and shadows this wider trend.

Concern with identity is, of course, but one explanatory proposition among others that claims to help clarify reasons for the pre-eminence of the body within contemporary social thought and popular culture. However, for cultural theorist, Fredric Jameson (1991), any explanation of late capitalism's love affair with the body has to be rooted in ideas concerning commodification. Here the argument is that capitalism, in its unquenchable thirst to make profits, is driven to find more and more things to *sell*, to make money from. If, therefore, we can be persuaded that our identity is bound up with the way our bodies are perceived in society, then there is money to be made – there is a market – out of altering those bodies and/or the perceptions that surround them. From this perspective, concern for the body and how it looks becomes less of an innocent and harmless preoccupation, and rather more tainted by the potentially murky world of markets and finance capital.

What connections are there – if any – between these social and cultural theories, Jacques Lecoq's school in Paris and the phenomenon of physical theatres? The reason for this short diversion into cultural theory is to suggest that we need to look both *within* and *outside* the structures of theatre-making in order to understand why a particular trend establishes itself at any given moment. Is it merely coincidence that, at a time of considerable growth in what has popularly been labelled *physical theatre*, there has also been a startling increase in our preoccupations with the body? To propose that this is more than mere coincidence is not to suggest that all those involved in the cultural practices of physical theatre are simple dupes, driven by forces they are neither conscious of, nor understand. Rather, it is to propose the notion that at least part of the reason for the growth of physical theatres – and associated institutions like Lecoq's school in Paris – is that they resonate with the 'temper of the times'. To put it slightly differently: the phenomenon of physical theatre articulates and expresses in all sorts of complex ways a wider interest in the human body and its significance in the world.

A presupposition that these various cultural theories share – and one which is particularly relevant to all forms of artistic activity – is that the human body is not a fixed biological, anatomical or 'god-given' entity. Rather, the body carries the traces of its own history – it 'speaks' of who we are. When we look at bodies – including our own – we see more than just flesh, hair, blood, muscles and so on. We see personal biography, the marks of suffering or happiness, and the imprint of class, gender, race and all those other characteristics and dispositions that make us who we are. This is an insight – an understanding – that lies at the heart of any theatre which chooses to foreground bodies, gestures and movement in its practice. Here, perhaps, a connection between the growth of physical theatre and those wider cultural forces identified above is most transparent. It is no coincidence, therefore, that the body has become a focus of attention in the work of, for example, certain black, gay or female theatre practitioners as a way of exploding and critiquing cultural preconceptions and prejudices. In live art and certain types of physical theatre, the body is regularly used to investigate the unspoken, the forgotten and the silenced, thus bringing marginalised or hitherto excluded experience to the foreground of the performance arena.

This part of the book has invited the reader to speculate momentarily upon theatre *in* society, and to consider some of the possible relationships between wider social forces at work in the contemporary world and physical theatre as one form of cultural production. The intention here has been temporarily to divert our focus away from the figure of Jacques Lecoq and to dwell briefly on a bigger picture in the hope that, by so doing, we have a clearer sense of the context into which his work needs to be located. To venture briefly down this avenue is not to diminish Lecoq's status within modern theatre, but to place his contribution upon a broader canvas so as to understand it better.

SUMMARY AND CONCLUSION

In this first chapter I have attempted to map out the defining features of Jacques Lecoq's life and work in theatre, and to place it historically and culturally within a larger context. I have suggested that, while his research and teaching into actor training and the role of movement within theatre have made a radical and particular contribution to twentieth-century Western performance, his practice can only be fully understood by locating it historically within other significant developments, and laterally in contemporary cultural thinking on the body.

Without proposing that there is an uncomplicated relationship between broader cultural thinking and specific artistic practices, I have argued that it is helpful to locate the *physical theatre* phenomenon, and hence Lecoq's contribution to these innovations in form and style, within that matrix of social and cultural thinking which has given pre-eminence to the body. Following Raymond Williams, I have indicated that a *cultural materialist* approach to understanding the phenomenon of body-based theatres is an essential accompaniment to a close 'textual' investigation of the forms themselves.

I have argued that Lecoq – sometimes explicitly, often implicitly – was responding to many of the same sorts of questions that other key figures engaged in twentieth-century actor training were also tackling. I have suggested, too, that, while Lecoq was clearly influenced by the practice of Copeau and Artaud, it is ultimately unhelpful to search for a 'definitive' legacy inherited from other earlier theatre practitioners. It is always important to recall Lecoq's background in sporting activities, and as a physiotherapist, when struggling to understand how he perceived the human body and its movement. His defining and abiding curiosity was always anchored in these two issues.

2

THE TEXTS OF
JACQUES LECOQ

My hope, perhaps utopian, is for my students to be consummate livers of life
and complete artists on stage.

(Lecoq 2000: 18)

This chapter examines the words of Jacques Lecoq in order to understand more fully what he thought about contemporary theatre, the
pursuit of acting and the *how* and *what* of his own teaching. Together,
these will enrich an appreciation of the man himself: his philosophy and
view of the world beyond the confines of the teaching studio. However,
as the quotation above implies, even to suggest a compartmentalisation
between his views on acting or teaching and life in its wider context is
misleading. Any close attention to Lecoq's utterances – written or
spoken – and to what close friends or colleagues have said about him,
indicates that there is an intimate, but complex, relationship between
the *how* and *what* of acting, for example, and his views on the way we
live – or might live – in the world. When reading *The Moving Body* or
watching the video, *Les Deux Voyages de Jacques Lecoq*, one is struck by a
curious combination of the practical and down-to-earth nature of his
approach on the one hand, and a willing recourse to the poetic, the
philosophical and the 'mystery of things' on the other. To notice these
latter qualities, however, is not to suggest that Lecoq claimed guru
status for himself, or indulged students who regarded their learning at

his school as either a spiritual quest or an experience of a therapeutic nature. As his writing makes abundantly clear, he had little sympathy for any of these positions. With some asperity, Lecoq remarks:

> exercises in group dynamics – e.g. holding hands before beginning a perform-
> ance – are very nice and helpful for the group. But not for a company of
> professional actors. . . . (I have heard that in Australia actors have their 'guru,'
> that in the United States they are attended by a 'shrink.') In Italy they go on
> stage and play. That's my idea, too.
>
> (2000: 69)

As I noted earlier in the book, Lecoq wrote comparatively little during his lifetime. Apart from *The Moving Body* and essays in *Le Théâtre du geste*, there is little else in the public domain, although shortly before his death he was apparently planning to collaborate with Simon McBurney, director of Théâtre de Complicité, on another book. In a conversation with the author, Fay Lecoq remarked that, although her husband had always been keen to document his ideas on theatre and teaching, he did not particularly enjoy writing, or find it an easy task. This is an ambiguity that perhaps is reflected in his affirmation of acquiring knowledge through *doing* – through practice – and its corollary, a low tolerance for 'book learning'.

Concentrating exclusively on three sources – *The Moving Body*, selected essays from *Le Théâtre du geste*, and a film for French television entitled *Les Deux Voyages de Jacques Lecoq*, made shortly before his death – this chapter focuses on two key questions: *how* did Lecoq teach and *what* did he teach. From these, and especially the *how* question, a picture emerges which also tells us a considerable amount about the man himself and his views on life, theatre and acting.

LECOQ'S PEDAGOGY: FROM PRACTICE TO PRINCIPLES (AND BACK)

Ultimately, it is impossible to detach form from content in Lecoq's teaching, just as it is an unattainable goal to separate these two elements when analysing a piece of live theatre or performance. The ability of any student to learn is as much to do with the effectiveness of the form or methodology of the teaching, as it is to do with how interesting or relevant the content appears to be. Nonetheless, it is a useful step within a longer journey to concentrate for a while on *how* Jacques Lecoq taught and his relationship with students, before we examine what areas of substance his teaching sought to interrogate.

NEITHER GURU NOR DIRECTOR

It is clear from his writing and from the comments of others that Lecoq sought to relate to his students neither as a director, nor as a spiritual *guru* or *master* dispensing unchallengeable wisdom about life and theatre:

> I am nobody. I am a neutral point through which you must pass in order to better articulate your own theatrical voice. I am only there to place obstacles in your path, so that you can better find your way around them.
>
> (2000: ix)

American theatre academic, Ron Jenkins, puts it another way and talks of 'Lecoq's self-effacing insistence that his students develop their own individual style of performance rather than imitate their teacher' (2001), while David Bradby notes that 'most unusually for a Parisian master, he rigorously excluded all cult of the personality, refusing even to publish the results of his researches until very late in life' (2002b: 92). On the school's thirtieth anniversary Lecoq erected a banner over the courtyard which read 'Don't do what I do. Do what you do' (Chamberlain and Yarrow 2002: 73). His position, however, is more complex than a face-value reading of these comments might suggest. While I am not proposing that there is bad faith to be detected in any of these observations, two of his ex-students, Andy Crook and Mark Evans, are more equivocal about the guru issue. Both Crook and Evans, who by chance were at the school at the same time in the early 1980s, have great regard and affection for Lecoq, but nonetheless point out that the force of his personality, his intellectual leadership of the school and the quality of his perception together gave him a quasi-guru status, whether he liked it or not. Without rancour, Crook observes:

> He did seem to be all knowing and all seeing. It was a very guru relationship and I find nothing wrong with that at all. . . . He said think for yourselves. Don't devalue yourselves. That would make him very angry. What great gurus do is offer questions, they don't provide answers. A guru throws it back at you. That's exactly what Jacques Lecoq did.
>
> (Crook 2002)

Moreover, it is certainly not a school that operates on a laissez-faire, 'anything goes' policy. Protocols regarding proper behaviour are strict, and perhaps the dividing line between respect for Lecoq's authority and fear of his criticism and disparagement was always a fine one. A clue to the subtleties of his relationship with students is suggested by this comment from the film profile – *Les Deux Voyages de Jacques Lecoq* – made by Jean-Noël Roy and Jean-Gabriel Carasso for French television. When responding to student work Lecoq says:

I don't try to do the staging. I try to see how it functions. So that they play better. So that they compose better. So that they can better stage themselves. So at the school there is always this curiosity to really know how things function, but I am not looking for interpretation, i.e. a director will interpret . . . he will give it his signature, whereas I remain simply amongst the motors that make things happen. . . . It's not knowledge which is transmitted identically to everybody. That's to say at the same time as there is this relationship between the professor and the students a transcendence is produced, i.e. something which is to be invented by one and the other.

(Roy and Carasso 1999)

We can extract a number of crucial points from this observation. First, Lecoq distinguishes between the response of the director and that of the teacher when witnessing student work. Second, his concern is to understand 'the motors that make things happen' – not the end result as such, but whether or not the student has found the most effective relationship between the disparate elements that go to make up a performance. Third, his pedagogy is predicated upon an assumption that knowledge cannot and should not be transmitted 'identically to everyone'. And, finally, he moves characteristically from the practical language of engineering – *the motors* – to the more mysterious chemistry which emerges from a successful teacher–student relationship, 'a transcendence . . . something which is invented by one and the other' (Figures 2.1 and 2.2).

As Chamberlain remarks in his introduction to *Jacques Lecoq and the British Theatre* he 'does not confuse the roles of teacher and director' (Chamberlain and Yarrow 2002: 9) and to understand this is critical in grasping the essence of Lecoq's approach to teaching. In this respect at least, it marks him out from virtually all the other great teacher-directors of modern theatre, such as Meyerhold, Copeau, Stanislavsky,

Grotowski and Barba, and goes some way towards explaining why the name of Lecoq is less well known than that of many comparable figures. The reason for this distinction lies in a belief which is central to Lecoq's philosophy – that is, to see the actor not as interpreter but as *creator*. Lecoq's school offers a method of working – a vocabulary shared by his graduates – which gives them access to a shared tool kit for making theatre and, if relevant, using text. Contrary to what outsiders sometimes imagine, in the second year Lecoq works with students on text, especially in the realms of tragedy and melodrama. When writing about his approach to tragic texts he observes:

> In our way of working, we enter a text through the body. We never sit around and discuss. . . . My teaching method steers clear of any interpretation, concentrating on the constant respect for the internal dynamics of the text, avoiding all *a priori* readings.

(Lecoq 2000: 137)

Like his metaphor of a mechanic working 'among the motors that make things happen' Lecoq talks here of 'respect for the internal dynamics' (of the text), thus again revealing a teaching approach which is concerned less with effects or products, and more with an in-depth examination of process and the mechanics of how things work. The

Figure 2.1 Jacques Lecoq in class (1995)

Figure 2.2 Jacques Lecoq (1972)

school, we are implicitly reminded, is a research laboratory and not an institution training would-be actors unquestioningly into accepted techniques and precepts. Interestingly, as a corollary to this concern with depth, Lecoq writes witheringly of the innumerable short workshops that are now a common feature in the landscape of performer training in Britain and elsewhere: 'unlike short courses, after which everyone kisses, sheds tears and promises to meet again, the school is a place of struggle, of tension and crises, out of which creativity is sometimes stimulated' (2000: 94). More specifically, he comments on 'the innumerable short workshops on clowning which are offered here and there, and which can only give a very superficial, reductive approach to work which needs to be prepared for in all the previous stages' (2000: 150).

VIA NEGATIVA

In *Jacques Lecoq and the British Theatre*, director and academic, John Wright, argues that Lecoq works largely through a form of *via negativa*, an approach which rejects prescription and illustration by example in favour of a search for the truth through negation. It was Grotowski who first used the phrase *via negativa* to describe an approach to learning which sought to eliminate inappropriate solutions and choices simply by saying 'no' to what the individual student or group had presented. In the *via negativa* prescriptions are not offered and it is up to the student to continue proposing possibilities until the most effective receives some kind of acceptance or affirmation. At its most extreme, this is a tough and ruthless pedagogy which less resilient students can find intimidating and morale-sapping. However, nowhere in the three main sources from which this chapter draws does Lecoq actually use the phrase *via negativa* to describe his method, and it is very unlikely that he drew upon Grotowski's approach in any deliberate way. Wright describes Lecoq's own particular take on this strategy:

> Lecoq uses the via negativa to manipulate creative energy. Sometimes he knows exactly what he wants his students to find and sometimes he simply uses it as a strategy to generate urgency; an atmosphere of white-hot discussion and experiment as his students struggle to find exactly what it is they think he is looking for. He plays a sophisticated game with his students and does not like them being too comfortable and confident.
>
> (Wright 2002: 73)

Philippe Gaulier, one-time teacher with Lecoq who has subsequently run his own school in both Paris and London, works in a similar way. The *via negativa* – or Lecoq and Gaulier versions of the same – is a demanding taskmaster and can sometimes yield no immediate results or solutions. From my own experience of spending a year (1986/7) training with Philippe Gaulier and Monika Pagneux at their Paris school, many 'results' of what I learned did not emerge or surface until years later. Often the body only understands and becomes able to articulate what it has learned long after the event itself. Lecoq suggests something similar in relation to his teaching of *commedia dell'arte*. Observing that, for young actors, a complete grasp of the territory of *commedia* is almost impossible because they have not lived long enough and therefore lack 'the tragic dimension', Lecoq goes on to say that, nonetheless 'we continue with this work at the school . . . so that students will retain a memory, both physical and mental, of this level of acting, and will be able to use it later' (Lecoq 2000: 116). Here, again, a rejection of immediate results and a concern with depth and long-term learning seems a crucial dimension of his pedagogy.

There is, perhaps, a curious tension between the technique of *via negativa* which, no matter how effective in the long term, can certainly be a harsh and demoralising experience in the lived moment of failure, and Lecoq's insistence on play – and the pleasure of play – as the motor of all creativity. Within the experience of, say, an *auto-cours* (see p. 60) which receives a negative response from tutors, probably the last emotions to register are pleasure and feelings of playfulness. The point here, however, is that, for Lecoq and Gaulier, the *pleasure of play* is not simply some kind of self-indulgent tomfoolery where having a wonderful time is the key to creativity and effective acting. Rather, an ability to play is more about *openness*, a readiness to explore the circumstances of the moment without intellectual 'editing', but within a set of rules or expectations germane to the style or form of theatre under investigation. Tough, therefore, as the *via negativa* experience may be for the student, for Lecoq and Gaulier it is often the absence of play – or a failure to play within the 'rules of the game' – which gives rise to a negative verdict. We will return to explore the issue of play in more detail later in this chapter.

I pursued the issue of *via negativa* with Thomas Prattki in conversation during a visit to the school in March 2002. Prattki confirmed that this approach was still used by many of the tutors, notwithstanding

Lecoq's death in 1999. For Prattki, the essential justification of *via nega-tiva* is that profound and substantial learning only takes place when students have discovered the most important things for themselves. Demanding though this technique undoubtedly is, the school believes it to be essential in creating an atmosphere of discovery in class: it invites pupils to accept responsibility for themselves. Significantly, Prattki also stressed that the injunction to 'discover' applied to the tutor as much as the student. Paraphrasing one of Lecoq's observations he said: 'I go into a class and I will leave them with something I did not know before. In any class I assume that the student will teach me some-thing' (Prattki 2002). Resonating with John Wright's argument, Prattki believes that, at its most successful – and in the right hands – *via negativa* is indeed a strategy to generate urgency and creative energy. Mark Evans well expresses the ambivalence that many Lecoq pupils are likely to have felt when on the receiving end of this approach to learning:

> I think for the students who can cope with it, it is a very provocative and chal-lenging way of teaching. It throws you back again and again into self-analysis, developing your own ability to observe. It created a great sense of anticipation, and actually the opposite of what you might imagine in that people were queuing up. . . . Of course, the pay-off is that, if and when you do get the praise, they have to squeeze your head out the door with a crowbar! But it did feel frustrating at times. You sometimes felt: why can't I understand intellectually, and then just do it?
>
> (Evans 2002)

ABSOLUTES, ESSENTIALS AND THE RICOCHET EFFECT

Another significant feature of Lecoq's pedagogical style, and one that must inevitably reflect a broader philosophical perspective, is his atti-tude towards absolutes and intellectual authority. We have already noted his rejection of the 'teacher as guru' paradigm for actor training, preferring instead an approach that implicitly repudiates the intellec-tual and emotional certainties associated with the idea of the great teacher as a 'master' who dispenses wisdom, knowledge and insight without question or challenge. Again, however, Lecoq refuses an un-ambiguous position for, at times, his writing speaks of *essentials*, the immutable and the permanent – especially when writing about nature and semi-mystical formulations like a 'universal poetic sense'. What is interesting here is that this very ambiguity offers scope for play and movement between opposites. In a fascinating passage at the beginning of *The Moving Body*, Lecoq articulates a philosophical position which seems at first to embrace certainty only then to undermine it with an honest acknowledgement of doubt and a delight in ambiguity. One senses a strong awareness – a celebration even – of the dynamic tension in this stance. Indeed, one might call it a kind of *playful* or teasing enjoyment of the contradictions inherent in a position which ultimately he has no choice but to occupy.

The following passage, quoted at some length, reveals Lecoq tussling with the absolute and the relative in relation to ideas about nature and the quest for neutrality. We will examine his work with the neutral mask later, but these words suggest that he clearly regards the attainment of some universal state of corporeal neutrality as an impossibility – as this extract indicates, it is the *journey* rather than the arrival which is important:

> We always return to the observation of nature and to human realities. I have a strong belief in permanency, in the 'Tree of trees', the 'Mask of masks', the balance that sums up perfect harmony. I realise that this tendency of mine may become an obstacle, but it is one that is necessary. Starting from an accepted reference point, which is neutral, the students discover their own point of view. Of course there is no such thing as absolute and universal neutrality, it is merely a temptation. This is why error is interesting. There can be no absolute without error. I am fascinated by the difference between the geographic pole and the magnetic pole. The North Pole does not quite coincide with true north. There is a small angle of difference, and it is lucky that this angle exists. Error is not just acceptable, it is necessary for the continuation of life, providing it is not too great. A large error is a catastrophe, a small error is essential for enhancing existence. Without error, there is no movement. Death follows.
>
> (Lecoq 2000: 20)

The importance that he ascribes to 'error' is crucial, both as a practical teaching strategy and as a philosophical disposition. Within the former it is about encouraging students to take risks, inviting them to fail and thus make discoveries which would never have been possible in an atmosphere that outlawed intellectual uncertainty and flexibility.

Nowhere is this more important than in the territory of clowning, where loss, vulnerability and 'not knowing' are the very preconditions for success and laughter. Philosophically, positively to embrace the possibility of error is to allow for movement, for *play*, for a departure from the norm, so as to be open to the new and the different. Lecoq writes engagingly about the 'ricochet effect' and the 'sideways approach' to teaching theatre: 'the whole school works indirectly: we never proceed in a straight line towards a student's desired goal' (Lecoq 2000: 53).

REFUSING AUTHORITY

Throughout *The Moving Body* there are many examples where Lecoq refuses the safety net of relying on a formal authority to validate his position, or what he is requiring from his students. This refusal takes a number of different forms, whether it be of theatrical or aesthetic traditions (e.g. *commedia dell'arte* and *bouffons*); reference books; technical and codified systems of mime; or athletic prowess for its own sake. His work on *commedia* and *bouffons* is not about rediscovering and then re-presenting these traditions for a modern audience, but about identifying key principles so as to *reinvent* them for the contemporary world. Reference books, he regularly reminds us, are of little help in this quest. For Lecoq, Étienne Decroux's Herculean task of developing a codified and formally structured system of modern mime, so that it can stand on its own proud feet as an independent art form, is not without interest, but ultimately such a project closes down and 'locks shut' any possible progress towards the rebirth of theatre. Despite a lifelong interest in sport, he rejects an approach that promotes fitness and athletic virtuosity for its own sake. Formalising and codifying movement techniques, whether via an athletic route, by the 'fixed dramatic forms of oriental theatre' (Lecoq 2000: 69) or through a grammar of modern mime, ultimately distort and stunt the creative development of young performers by denying them the possibility of *play*. The training provided for athletes and for those apprenticed in the codified forms of Eastern dance dramas:

> often insufficiently practised, set up physical circuits in the actor's body, which then become difficult to justify, especially when the actor is young. In these cases, actors only retain the outer, aesthetic form.

> (Lecoq 2000: 69)

One might say that Lecoq's whole teaching project represents a rejection of acting as an 'outer, aesthetic form' and in this he finds common cause with, for example, Stanislavsky, Meyerhold, Michael Chekhov, Grotowski and even Decroux – all figures who, in other crucial respects, might seem strange intellectual bedfellows. His phrase 'physical circuits in the actor's body' also reveals a significant insight into the role of physiology, the musculature and body memory for the performer. Here the consequence of movement work or physical training for the actor is not a set of external techniques and skills which can be turned on and off according to need and circumstance. Far more importantly, it is the implanting of new 'physical circuits' in the performer's body – movement patterns that become incorporated through and into the musculature, and hence begin to shape the actor's bodily disposition in the world. Lecoq's interest in the kind of physical circuits implanted in the body through training relates closely to another term – *le dépôt* – which provides a crucial key to his thinking about the relationship between movement and memory. Like a number of other words that are central to his teaching vocabulary there is no precise equivalent for *le dépôt* in the English language. Clearly, the closest translation is 'deposit', but also 'depot' as in 'storehouse' provides a useful insight into how Lecoq uses the term. Dick McCaw, who worked with Lecoq on a number of projects for the International Workshop Festival, shared with him an interest in geology. In a conversation McCaw discussed with me Lecoq's use of the term *le dépôt*:

> He would say 'le geste c'est le dépôt d'une emotion' [crudely translatable as 'gesture is the deposit of an emotion']. But how to translate the word *dépôt*? I suggested that it was a bit like a river with gradual sedimentation . . . the result of movement against rock, of water against the bank. It's not like an essence, not some Platonic idea. Through the regular use of a gesture, there's a gradual accretion.

(McCaw 2002)

David Bradby takes the idea further: 'He believed that the ability to respond creatively, or poetically, depended on the laying down, as it were, of a series of sediments through our experience of the universally shared experiences' (Bradby 2002b: 86). These are clearly complex – and perhaps controversial – ideas at the centre of which can be found propositions about the relationship between an individual's body memory and a shared universal sense of common experiences which are particular to the human species. The concept of *le dépôt* takes us into the arena of the neutral mask where, in order for the actor to achieve a state of creative openness, he or she has to rediscover a range of basic experiences through the world of movement, sound, shapes, textures and colours.

Lecoq's concern about the impact on the actor of certain kinds of training regimes is that they may deliberately or inadvertently lock shut the possibility of further creative development. This is really the touchstone upon which his whole relationship with other 'authorities' was based. It is not that he had little respect for different theatre traditions. Indeed, his preoccupation with the dramatic territories of tragedy, the chorus, *commedia* and melodrama provides palpable evidence to the contrary. The point he is making is that any form of physical training begins to 'reprogramme' the body and thus modify and embellish *body memory*. There is no choice here. It cannot be avoided, because this is what happens when bodies are subjected to physical training regimes. The critical question, however, is *which* training systems and for *what* purpose are they being taught? It is also, as Lecoq suggests in the comment quoted above, an issue about depth and superficiality.

ANTI-INTELLECTUALISM

A charge that has been levelled against Lecoq from time to time is that of *anti-intellectualism*, and together some characteristics of his teaching methodology may seem to add substance to the accusation. An apparent rejection of books as a source of learning, a disdain for accepted authority figures, the injunction to students that they should learn through *doing* rather than talking and discussion, and a disposition towards enjoying popular theatre forms such as the clown and melodrama: all these when cast in a particular light may give credence to the charge. The reality, I would argue, is rather different and can only have much validity if one accepts a narrow definition of what constitutes 'an intellectual'. Certainly, there is some evidence that Lecoq had little time for what he regarded as a pretentious (over)theorising of art or theatre practice, and, certainly, there was often delight in the apparent purity of a simple, uncomplicated gesture or action. Moreover, he had little patience with the proposition that theatre should be first and foremost a cerebral endeavour. As Fay Lecoq points out: 'he never had any time for French *intellectual* theatre which he felt was dreadful . . . two actors sitting on chairs . . . just talking heads' (Fay Lecoq 2001).

However, if a defence is necessary against the charge of being anti-intellectual, even a brief examination of Lecoq's working life for nearly fifty years reveals the limitations of such a claim. In that his school functioned as much as a *laboratory* as it did a training institution or academy, and in that Lecoq devoted much of his life to *thinking* about the nature of the relationship between movement and acting, then the charge is easily dismissed. Similarly, those who latch upon Lecoq's scepticism about reference books as proof of anti-intellectualism are failing to read his words carefully. He says that 'no reading of reference books can substitute for creative work, renewed each day in the school' (Lecoq 2000: 98). The argument here is that, for a pedagogy which aspires to prepare actors for the theatre – rather than, for example, to train sociologists, historians or cultural theorists – book learning can never be a *substitute for creative work*. This, surely, is the point at stake: not a risible rejection of book learning per se; merely a firm emphasis that such an approach is of secondary importance in the process of learning to act – a course of action that is first and foremost a somatic and corporeal one.

In an interview with me, David Bradby, who has written extensively about contemporary French theatre and cultural life, remarked that he had always been perplexed by the lack of recognition accorded to Lecoq within his own lifetime by fellow French theatre-makers and commentators. He had noted that, on Lecoq's death, some of the obituaries in the French national press were slightly grudging in their acknowledgement of his importance, with *Le Monde* in particular proposing that his work had been useful for the 'Anglo-Saxons', but of less value for the French themselves. Lecoq, Bradby suggests in a book of essays entitled *The Paris Jigsaw*, 'was viewed by those in the Paris theatre establishment as an unorthodox outsider' (2002b: 89). Assuming that this was indeed the case, one imagines Lecoq being singularly unperturbed by such a perception. Fay Lecoq confirmed this point to me, but was also anxious to point out that, behind any such public front, her husband was also a touch hurt and saddened by the failure of the French cultural establishment to recognise his achievements and discoveries, notwithstanding his award of the Legion d'honneur in April 1982. If there was a degree of indifference to Lecoq's work from French academics, this was partially due to the belief that he was 'anti-intellectual'. Lecoq's school took root and began to flourish during a period when French intellectual life was dominated by a number of highly theoretical thinkers about cultural forces – Louis Althusser, Jacques Derrida, Jean Baudrillard, Jacques Lacan and Michel Foucault as just some of the most prominent examples. As Bradby put it, 'he was not theoretical in a country that values theory over practice' (2002a).

Perhaps the most interesting element of this debate is that it reveals a way of thinking about the intellect which is predicated upon an assumption that separates mind from body, thinking from doing and feeling from movement. If Lecoq enjoined his students to learn through action, the senses and somatic experiences, rather than through talk and reading books, this does not make him 'anti-intellectual'. Rather, it suggests a perspective which proposes that learning can only ever be successful if it works on the assumption of an integrated mind–body, or indeed a human species where mind and body are but one.

THE GARDEN AND THE JOURNEY: LECOQ'S USE OF IMAGERY

Another clue towards identifying Lecoq's pedagogical style, and the philosophical assumptions that provide a frame for the school's work, is to consider his use of language and the kind of metaphors he regularly called upon to illuminate and explain his ideas. In a section where he describes how his teaching invokes the dynamic and textural qualities of elements, materials and animals in order to explore character, Lecoq writes that the 'language of analogy is both rich and precise and goes beyond any psychological approach' (Lecoq 2000: 87). It is noticeable that, throughout his writing and when interviewed, he employs a language which is richly littered with metaphor and analogy. Apart from an evident delight in the geological metaphor (strata, sediment, deposit), images of travel and of gardening seem to surface regularly. Combining both, he writes that 'in the course of the first year we shall have planted the roots, enriched the soil, turned over the earth. We shall have completed three journeys' (2000: 97). Elsewhere, Lecoq comments elliptically on how he sees his relationship with the students:

I don't want my pupils to love me. Good and evil don't exist in teaching, nor do prescriptions, only analysis of how things move. I'm like a gardener who knows how to make a carrot grow better than others. But I could never turn it into a turnip.

(Hiley 1988)

The image of theatre teacher as gardener coaxing growth from his young seeds or shoots is a poetic if slightly predictable metaphor for the learning process. However, it is not too fanciful, I feel, to regard these figures of speech as more than a rather florid linguistic device. Given the great importance which Lecoq placed on the necessity of his students studying 'life' and the movements of nature – not simply for some abstract notion of moral or aesthetic worth, but because this process helped them to grasp the essentials of movement – these horticultural images serve an analytical as well as a literary purpose.

More significant than the gardening imagery, Lecoq's use of the *journey* as a constant metaphor and source of inspiration and provocation for his work seems a more revealing use of language. References to journeys abound in *The Moving Body* and the title of the two film profiles made by Roy and Carasso – *Les Deux Voyages de Jacques Lecoq* – mirrors his own use of the word to describe the students' passage over two years at the school. It is clear, however, that these are never-ending journeys – there is no closure or conclusion in the learning or developmental process encountered by the students. They will finish certain parts of the course and ultimately leave the school, but learning is never complete. In an obvious way Lecoq's use of the word *journey* signifies a perpetual sense of movement – a state of being that echoes *Tout bouge* (*Everything Moves*), the title of his lecture-demonstration performed across the world on many occasions from the late 1960s. That there is no arrival in this pedagogical journey presents – according to one's disposition – either a nightmare scenario of endless existential uncertainty, or one of perpetual openness and a delight in discovery. Again, while the learning process as journey is hardly an original formulation, there is something more to his use of the metaphor than wishing to convey a feeling of movement and openness. There is a sense that, for Lecoq, an interest in the concept of travelling – of journeying – is more than the pleasure of alighting on a neat metaphor; it emerges from the experience and preoccupations of a young man growing up to observe the cataclysmic upheavals of the Second World War and its aftermath in Europe. For anyone of Lecoq's generation – raised in the heart of Europe – the Nazi occupation of France and the subsequent displacement of peoples throughout the continent must have scored a graphic mark on the bodies of all those around to witness such events. In *Les Deux Voyages* Lecoq reflects on his own journey since 1945:

> The idea of travel, of displacement has always been something that interested me. I must say that I marvel in the journey through the life of things. And in the theatre I like to say it's an attentive trip. I like Dante's voyage . . . I like that a lot.
>
> (Roy and Carasso 1999)

It is no coincidence that the third theme for first-year students' *autocours* is that of *The Exodus*, which Lecoq remarks:

> was very poignant in the post-war years and is now finding new echoes. . . . All types of exodus appear: migration from the countryside to the towns, refugees fleeing war and bombs, etc. In this way the students can project contemporary concerns onto an imaginary realm which is of global significance.
>
> (Lecoq 2000: 92)

Similarly, within the second-year exploration of melodrama he remarks that time is a key factor in structuring this form, and that the two principal themes which most resonate within this territory are *The Return* and *The Departure*. Students are invited to work on a scenario entitled 'The Departure for America', which, Lecoq remarks, 'raises the great theme of exile' (2000: 106). From the Sicilian peasant leaving Palermo with a single suitcase for the New World in the 1930s, a more contemporary context is suggested when students work from the image of the African worker who has left his country for France to earn enough of a living to feed the family he has left behind.

From these examples we can see that Lecoq's use of *journey* as a key image is more than just a helpful linguistic prop. For the alert student and anyone concerned with understanding and identifying the *motors* that drove his thinking and teaching, we can observe that Lecoq's employment of the metaphor leads us back to his experiences as a young man growing to maturity during and immediately after the Second World War. It also signposts a subtle but pervasive politics that shades all his work: a preoccupation with – and commitment to – *internationalism*. We shall return to the issue later in this chapter.

SCHOOL, CURRICULUM AND STUDENTS

To conclude this part of my exploration of *how* Lecoq approached his teaching, I want to consider the overall relationship between the Paris school and its students. It is clear that Lecoq's relationship with his students was a complex one. 'I don't want my pupils to love me', he said (see extract on p. 58), and one has a strong impression that he was completely uninterested in courting popularity. For all his passion and astute ability to diagnose the strengths and weaknesses of each student, one senses a formal distance deliberately sustained between tutor and the taught. Not for Lecoq the jokey banter and camaraderie that some theatre teachers try to foster with their pupils. As we have seen, he has no time for an approach to pedagogy that encourages a cosy atmosphere of mutual support through handholding, group hugging or other quasi-therapeutic approaches.

And yet . . . and yet, Lecoq insists that '[i]t is essential to have fun and our school is a happy school. Not for us, tortured self-questioning about the best way to walk on stage: it is enough that it be done with pleasure' (2000: 65). It is clear too that, if he demanded a relationship of some distance with students, this did not mean that he never listened to them. Indeed, the history of the school's development since 1957 is punctuated by Lecoq identifying and responding to the undercurrents of student interest and preoccupation at particular junctures. The most graphic example of this was the introduction of the *auto-cours* during the student rebellions of 1968 in Paris and other capital cities across the Western world. Simon McBurney recalls the actress Celia Gore-Booth, who trained with Lecoq in the late 1960s, talking about these events and their impact on the school:

> even the pupils in his school were affected by '68 and like a lot of students at that time they turned over the whole school and they refused to work. And they said to Lecoq, we don't want to work, we want to teach ourselves. And Lecoq, who's the constant responder and observer, said: every day for an hour you will teach yourselves. And it was called *auto-cours*.

(McBurney 1994: 19)

Auto-cours, however, was more than a temporary and expedient response to the extraordinary circumstances of the late 1960s. Since that time it has become a central part of the curriculum and – arguably –

one of the defining characteristics of the school. Thus, within the current timetable ninety minutes is devoted to groups of students preparing short pieces of performance on a given theme that they will present in front of the whole school at the end of each week.

It would be wrong to imagine that *auto-cours* simply expresses those quintessential freedom-loving and self-determining qualities supposedly typical of the 1960s. It is a demanding teaching tool, not only in terms of having to work effectively and collaboratively with people whom Simon McBurney wryly notes 'you absolutely hated' (1994: 18), but also because of critical feedback from Lecoq and other tutors. Until witnessing a day of first year *auto-cours* performances when visiting the school in March 2002, I had not gauged the degree of formality with which these performances are presented and received. Apart from being open to all the school's pupils, other guests and invited professionals, the work will be evaluated by a team of tutors who closely observe each performance. Thus, on the occasion of my visit, the Director of Pedagogy, Thomas Prattki, led the tutors' critique. On several occasions, shapeless or poorly conceived work was stopped before its completion and the student group subjected to a fair, but rigorously astringent, analysis from the team of tutors. The most successful pieces won considerable affirmation, not in terms of praise for individual performances, but for the quality of the choices made in relation to component elements such as rhythm, observation, play and timing. One piece, set in a library, was highly praised by Prattki and his colleagues with phrases like 'well constructed', 'very simple' and 'great detail'. Here, Prattki went to considerable lengths to identify the use of bodily imbalance that added powerfully to visual and comic appeal – 'when the body is out of balance it is interesting and engaging'. Lecoq contrasted the purpose of *auto-cours* with other elements of the curriculum: 'unlike improvisation work which deals mainly with acting, the work done in *auto-cours* emphasises production, playwriting and also the necessity of collaborative work in the theatre' (Lecoq 2000: 92).

Another area which has found its permanence in the curriculum, at least partly as a consequence of listening to the students, is that of the clowns. Lecoq introduced the subject in the 1960s when he was considering the relationship between *commedia dell'arte* and circus clowns. Realising very rapidly the limitations of the genre of circus clowning for theatre, he began – unexpectedly almost – to investigate what lay at the core of this form of humour. Lecoq admits to being sustained on this path of enquiry by the enthusiasm shown for the subject by his students – a path, it is curious to note, which covers a very similar territory of interest to one of those trodden by Samuel Beckett. Lecoq observed: 'today I notice that the students are always asking to work on clowns and consider it one of the high points of the school's educational journey' (2000: 149). He ascribes this interest as being deeply rooted in a quest for liberation from the 'social masks' we all wear, and hence to come to terms with the more ridiculous – and therefore vulnerable – dimensions of our personality. While to certain observers clown work can sometimes seem irritatingly 'twee' and precious, for Lecoq and Gaulier it has at its heart a subversive and radical dimension which chimed with the spirit of 1968. Mark Evans makes the point that 'there is a politics to play and to the clown, as in some respects they could be seen as offering space for the body to be *unruly* [my emphasis] – to break away from the docility of training' (Evans 2002).

For Lecoq, listening to his students was as much an integral aspect of his daily research as observing the bustle of multicultural life in and around rue du Faubourg St Denis. His relationship over time to the students who passed through the school mirrored the ambiguity we have already noted in Lecoq's approach to philosophical universals, between change and stability, between the alternating allure and threat of uncertainty. In describing his relationship with students, he implies that the encounter is often one of struggle:

> The great strength of the school lies in its students. They are constantly thrown back on themselves and have to invent their own theatre. We may suggest themes, offer advice, stimulate the students by imposing restraints, but we can never go any deeper until they are engaged by the work. Nevertheless, students are often contradictory. *We must hear what they say without listening too much* [my emphasis]. We must also grapple with them if we are to lead them into a place of true poetry.
>
> (Lecoq 2000: 23)

We must hear what they say without listening too much: a neat formulation which well conveys Lecoq's ability to respect his students at a deep level without ever feeling the need either to court their popularity, or to respond to every passing fad and foible they might express. The school changed and developed under Lecoq's leadership – 'the school is in a state of constant movement and continues to develop'

He lent grace . . .

- He was fully attentive to the transformation of each actor, each student. He lent grace to the individual's own personality. He was capable of pushing around a personality then afterwards leaving it alone, letting it go free.

  (Dario Fo in Roy and Carasso 1999)

- His way of teaching – the very concrete way in which he wanted the body to treat poetry. His down to earth style . . . that showed me a certain truth which is not to imagine that everything takes place in the head . . . the theatre is flesh. It's from the verb made flesh and Lecoq transmits that.

  (Ariane Mnouchkine in Roy and Carasso 1999)

- The taste for form in theatre came to me through the work of Jacques Lecoq, and that even the instantaneous is a form. There were so many passionate things about Lecoq – a kind of alchemy and knowledge . . . a profound knowledge of certain laws, of certain poetic laws of the theatre.

  (Luc Bondy in Roy and Carasso 1999)

- He was interested in creating a site to build on, not a finished edifice. Contrary to what people often think, he had no style to propose. He offered no solutions. He only posed questions.

  (McBurney 1999a)

- Lecoq always seemed to me an impossible man to approach. . . . It always amazed me – his ability to make you feel completely ignored and then, afterwards, make you discover things about yourself that you never knew were there. That distance made him great. It was nice to think that you would never dare to sit at his table in Chez Jeanette to have a drink with him.

  (Valdez 1999: 8)

(2000: 13) – but clearly these changes were either a consequence of quiet and measured reflection, or emerged, seamlessly as it were, through minute transformations of the daily teaching process. Lecoq put it like this: 'we do not turn great somersaults, we are like the sea: the movement of the waves above is more visible than the currents beneath, but despite that there is movement in the depths' (2000: 13).

ACTING FOR THE THEATRE OF THE FUTURE

The second part of this chapter shifts focus away from the *how* of Lecoq's teaching towards what he believed were the components of effective acting, and – by implication – successful theatre. As has been emphasised throughout this account so far, Lecoq had little interest in simply equipping his students with 'technical' acting skills for the existing theatre. Across all his writing he speaks often – either directly or by implication – of 'the new young theatre which I hope to see come into existence' (Lecoq 2000: 161). One of the elusive and paradoxical qualities of Lecoq's vision was that it was at once both radical and at least partially rooted in 'permanence' and in what he believed were the 'universal laws of theatre'. What follows begins to untangle some of these tensions and signpost areas for further study. Here, rather than simply retrace all those components of his work which Lecoq explains so thoroughly in *The Moving Body*, I have attempted to identify and interrogate core principles, themes and issues in his teaching, and for the actor's preparation for this 'new young theatre'.

If any one term encapsulates Lecoq's overall goal for his students during the two years they may study with him, it is that of *preparation*: preparing the creative actor. Compared to the more circumscribed word 'training', *preparation* seems to imply a process of getting ready, of open-endedness and an unwillingness to close down on possible options and choices. Perhaps, *preparation* also suggests a productive relationship with 'creativity', whereas the formulation 'training for creativity' seems almost a contradiction in terms – certainly a liaison where the two components are pulling in opposing directions. The four areas I will now examine – play, *disponibilité* and *complicité*; mime and movement; the quest for neutrality; and understanding the dynamics of space – all may be considered as vital components of this preparation. They are more than this too, for all connect in one way or another to what Lecoq calls the main *dramatic territories* of melodrama, *commedia dell'arte*, tragedy, *bouffons* and the clown, and are vital elements of the motors which drive each of these forms. The practical exercises presented in the book's final chapter offer ways for students to move from physical preparation, through improvisation and into these dramatic territories.

LE JEU, DISPONIBILITÉ AND *COMPLICITÉ*

In the order presented, these words may be crudely translated as: play or playfulness; openness or availability; and rapport or a spirit of the 'accomplice'. The latter quality is critical in the achievement of a true sense of ensemble. English translations, however, do little justice to the complexity and subtlety of these ideas, especially when pursued through practice by Lecoq.

Le jeu

The quality and concept of *play* recurs throughout *The Moving Body*, and – by all accounts – peppered his daily dialogue with students. Lecoq defines play like this: 'when, aware of the theatrical dimension, the actor can shape an improvisation for spectators, using rhythm, tempo, space, form' (Lecoq 2000: 29). Unpicking this definition, we can highlight three concepts in particular: *theatricality*, *improvisation* and *spectators*. Being 'aware of the theatrical dimension' removes play or playfulness from mere pleasurable self-indulgence and provides it with context and purpose. To 'shape an improvisation' suggests territory where the actor has a degree of physical, vocal and spatial freedom to be inventive, rather than being merely a conduit for the director or playwright. Invoking the presence of spectators in this definition reminds the actor that finding this elusive quality of play is a crucial – perhaps the most crucial – element in making the transaction between performers and audience effective and engaging. Without play – in its richest and most nuanced form – spectators will never be properly engaged in the theatrical event. This belief is integral to the teaching of both Lecoq and Philippe Gaulier and to all their 'disciples'. While the notion of play finds its lineage in Copeau and Meyerhold, as both concept and practice it is Lecoq and Gaulier who have most explored its form, texture and component elements.

Play

- An actor can only truly play when the driving structure of the written play allows him to do so.

  (Lecoq 2000: 99)

- The technical mastery of all these acrobatic movements, falls and jumps, has in reality a single aim: to give greater freedom to the player.

  (ibid.: 71)

- Beyond styles or genres we seek to discover the *motors of play*.

  (ibid.: 98)

- My method aims to promote the emergence of a theatre where the actor is playful

  (ibid.: 98)

- The main criterion for selection (into the second year) is the actor's capacity for play

  (ibid.: 2000: 97)

For Lecoq, the performer who cannot play can never be a creative actor. An ability to play, in other words, is a necessary condition for creativity. He writes about the 'virtuosity and pleasure of play' being the 'most important dimensions of acting' (2000: 65). For Philippe Gaulier, a four-week course entitled *Le Jeu* is the first in a sequence of programmes which students can take separately, and in any order. However, *Le Jeu* underpins everything else, and is the one course without which a student would be ill-equipped to tackle all the main dramatic territories explored throughout the rest of his teaching programme. Gaulier extols the *pleasure* of play to his students, at the same time as demanding a *lightness* that he believes to be an essential component to the challenge of playing. For both Lecoq and Gaulier, an ability to play is as indispensable for the performing of tragedy as it is to clowning or other – apparently – less serious genres of theatre.

Discovering that the spirit of play when performing *King Lear*, *Medea* or *A Long Day's Journey into Night* is as important as in any farce or comedy is often difficult for students to grasp. Play, with all its attendant meanings, is indeed a deceptively complex issue for the actor to understand and embody.

Former Lecoq student, Alan Fairbairn, adds another dimension to what is meant by *play* at the school:

> The whole notion of *play* is essential to Lecoq's school. The most important element of *play* . . . always seemed to be connected with making the most of whatever material was available theatrically when you were on stage at any particular moment. I think *play* is about rendering the moment on stage into life – bringing it alive – exploiting the moment.
>
> (cited in Murray 2002: 32)

Here, *play* seems to be about the possibility of enriching the available meanings around any particular piece of theatrical business, whether with objects, script or another performer. This is the territory where making a cup of tea, smoking a cigarette or moving a chair, for example, can be explored – physically – in any number of ways. This is also the terrain that connects us laterally to certain elements of live or performance art, where the handling and exploration of materials and objects may be central to the performative process. **Tim Etchells** (1962–), director and writer with British performance company, *Forced Entertainment*, extols the importance of play in work very different from that which we associate with artists trained by Lecoq and Gaulier:

> It [play] is an attempt to shift the boundaries of real time and real space. Play is looser than games – it has a chameleon-like, mutable quality. It allows a shift of rules, a shift between different positions – an 'I can change the paradigm we are working in' quality. If you ditch psychological narrative in performance it's easy to lose the sense that anything is happening. Play (and competition) are useful in that they can make dynamic what might otherwise be a purely presentational image.
>
> . . .
>
> Play is a state in which meaning is flux, in which possibility thrives, in which versions multiply, in which the confines of what is real are blurred, buckled, broken.
>
> (Etchells 1995)

Surprisingly, perhaps, it also suggests historical connections with Stanislavsky's investigation of physical actions. In contrast to his better-known 'system', Stanislavsky's later work developed a rehearsal technique which proposed that emotions could be more easily generated through intensive physical work on a character's actions. Here, like Lecoq, the route to emotional truth is from the outside in. Play raises difficult questions, too, in relation to dramaturgy. When, for example, does inventive play around, say, making a cup of tea exceed the intended meanings of the action? At what point does 'inventive play' degenerate into self-conscious cleverness and virtuosity? It is this dimension of play – this *misuse* of play – which has given rise to criticism which claims that physical theatre sometimes represents a triumph of style or form over substance and meaning. Play can be risky territory in the hands of an undisciplined actor, or an indulgent director.

If we scrutinise Lecoq's writing closely we find another crucial dimension to play, and one that is less often remarked upon by commentators. Nevertheless, it illustrates a very important element within his theory of acting, and also invites us to encounter one of those paradoxes or tensions in which Lecoq seems to delight. Here, Lecoq offers a meaning to play that resembles usage as in 'the play of a bicycle chain' – in other words, where there is enough slack or flexibility to allow for movement and freedom. If there is no play in a chain or piece of rope, it is taut, inflexible and liable to brittleness. For the actor, therefore, there has to be a relationship to the character he or she is representing which has a degree of *play* or *distance* in it. Lecoq puts it without equivocation:

> If character becomes identical with personality there is no play. It may be possible for this kind of osmosis to work in the cinema, in psychological close-ups, but theatre performance must be able to make an image carry from stage to spectator. There is a huge difference between actors who express their own lives, and those who can truly be described as players.

(Lecoq 2000: 61)

This statement is of great significance in understanding Lecoq's position on acting, as it seems at once to create distance, on the one hand, from early Stanislavskian theories that rest on psychological motivation and emotional identification and, on the other hand, from some perspectives on contemporary performance where representation is to be replaced by the quest for presence and 'being oneself'. It also suggests that the process of acting for the camera is very different from one that positions the performer in front of a live audience. For Lecoq, success in the live performer–audience transaction is dependent upon being able 'to make an image carry from stage to spectator'.

Lecoq takes this argument further in other parts of his book, where he argues the need for distance between an actor's strongly held personal or political beliefs and the role that is being presented. 'I prefer to see more distance between the actor's own ego and the character performed. This allows the performer to play even better', he says, adding: 'actors usually perform badly in plays whose concerns are too close to their own' (2000: 19). From my own training with Philippe Gaulier, I can remember him saying much the same thing, although perhaps even more vehemently. For both Lecoq and Gaulier, a strong political identification with either role or the central meanings of the piece in question is likely to remove that necessary distance, the *play* required in the bicycle chain. This position raises questions about how then to perform politically committed theatre. Neither man would self-evidently wish to embargo such work, and indeed Lecoq's quietly radical politics surface throughout his writing, and in *Les Deux Voyages*. However, for Lecoq, a theatre which articulates a strong politics still requires a playful distance between personality and role if it is to be effective and persuasive.

If there is a paradox inherent in Lecoq's views on play it lies in the tension between the necessity of achieving – at the same time – both engagement and distance. Play or playfulness is only possible if the performer is fully present in the moment – the physical action, for example – but successful play opens up space that in turn creates the necessary distance between actor and role for an effective engagement to take place with an audience. Play, therefore, lies at the heart of Lecoq's views on theatre and acting. Through his teaching, play is a complex and demanding proposition for the student. While the pleasurable dimension of playing – as in the child playing – is central to the process, it is only part of the story. The student who plays too hard – who tries to play too much – ends by failing to establish that distance which is a necessary condition for effective acting.

Disponibilité and complicité

Although they hardly feature in *The Moving Body* — and find no place in the glossary — *disponibilité* and *complicité* are also key terms in Lecoq's pedagogical vocabulary. Dictionary translations into English do scant justice to the qualities Lecoq is searching for when he employs these terms. As ideas and states they are clearly from the same family as *play* or *le jeu*, and indeed are mutually interdependent for their realisation. One might say that *disponibilité* is a precondition for play, while *complicité* is an outcome of successful play.

Although Lecoq does not offer the following phrase as a definition of *disponibilité*, it comes as close as possible to describing what it takes for the actor to be *disponible*. In writing about the function of the neutral mask, he says: 'it puts him in a state of discovery, of openness, of freedom to receive' (2000: 38). This quality is not peculiar to work with the neutral mask, but is most obviously a precondition for success in this area. Indeed, it is hard to imagine any teacher of acting or performance not wanting students to be *disponible*. The quality, therefore, is not peculiar to Lecoq's teaching, but is certainly strongly emphasised, especially in its relation to *play*. However, while the more conventional drama teacher would see this spirit of availability largely in terms of psychological or emotional openness, for Lecoq it is through the body and movement that one finds the route to achieve such a quality. This perspective should remind us of an important issue raised briefly in the first chapter of this book, namely that implicit in all Lecoq's work is an attack on the dualism espoused by the philosopher, **René Descartes** (1596–1650): a position which presupposes a body separate and disconnected from mind and spirit. Like many of the great twentieth-century theatre teachers, Lecoq's pedagogy – almost at every stage – challenges this separation. Hence, in the quest for the *disponible* actor, physical work on the body which aims, for example, to free it from unnecessary tensions and render it more supple and flexible, is at the same time helping to induce a spirit of psychological or emotional openness. These are not two different compartments of the human species that need to be tackled separately: by working physically with the actor one is also working mentally. The *disponible* actor does not need to be an athlete or a gymnast, but it is almost impossible to imagine such a quality in any performer who is physically closed and corporeally unresponsive.

The spirit or condition of *complicité* has been brought into the cultural foreground by Théâtre de Complicité, the London-based, but resolutely international, theatre company. One imagines that, when founder members of the company left the Lecoq school in the early 1980s *complicité* was one of the qualities they most aspired to achieve in their work. To understand the term we need to look beyond a straight dictionary translation into English. The idea of *complicité* takes us into two separate but related territories: the quality of ensemble, and the nature of the performer–audience relationship. In Théâtre de Complicité's programmes for *The Visit* and *The Three Lives of Lucy Cabrol*, a meaning for the term is offered which seems to capture two of its key qualities. *Complicité* is a 'form of collusion between celebrants' writes Michael Ratcliffe in the programme notes for *The Three Lives of Lucy Cabrol* in 1994. *Collusion* and *celebrants*: two words which tell us much about Théâtre de Complicité's approach to making theatre and the spirit of Jacques Lecoq. Here, I sense, that *collusion* suggests much more than the anodyne and neutral 'working together' or 'cooperation'. There is something slightly dark and suspicious about the term, implying perhaps a landscape where rules and laws are transgressed, and where boundaries are tested and extended – not for some wicked purpose, but in a spirit of shared, gleeful pleasure: more the camaraderie of rogues and revolutionaries, than the quiet, self-satisfied handholding of saints. Hence, the more appropriate *celebrants* rather than the purely descriptive *actors* or *performers*. Here, too, we are led back to Lecoq's fundamental belief in 'the pleasure of play'.

True ensemble is not ultimately about the ability of, say, fifteen performers to remember their lines, listen to cues, reach an agreed spot on stage at the precise moment, or to keep tightly in time with each other during a dance or movement routine. The spirit of ensemble only communicates itself to an audience when there is a palpable sense of those performers all being *complicit* – of colluding – in the deed of daring to create and present a show to spectators. In describing how the company makes its work, members talk about a process of 'collective imagining', a state that is only possible, one supposes, if it is prefigured by a genuine *complicité*.

Le jeu, *disponibilité* and *complicité* present a triad of qualities – elusive and almost impossible to constrain by tight definitions – which Lecoq is searching for among his students. For him, they are essential qualities in successful acting and – by implication – for the 'theatre of tomorrow'.

THE QUEST FOR NEUTRALITY

- The first year is a year of demystification of ready-made ideas.

  (Lecoq 1973: 41)

- In our work, the search for self-enlightenment and spiritual bliss has little attraction. The ego is superfluous.

  (Lecoq 2000: 19)

- When a student has experienced this neutral starting point his body will be freed, like a blank page on which drama can be inscribed.

  (ibid.: 36)

- The neutral mask is not a symbolic mask.

  (ibid.: 38)

- [The neutral mask] is always in 'a state of equilibrium'.

  (Wright 2002: 76)

- By making no comment or by 'having no story', the neutral mask creates a vacuum that, as an audience, our imaginations rush to fill.

  (ibid.)

- It's a way of looking at the world, the neutral mask. It's a necessary passage.

  (ibid.)

- Through the neutral mask, Lecoq is trying to return his student to the precognitive state, where he is free to gather fresh mimic impressions.

  (Felner 1985: 158)

- At the moment of neutral action, one does not know what one will do next, because anticipation is a mark of personality.

  (Eldredge and Huston 1995: 123)

- The neutral mask is a way of understanding performance, not a way of performing.

  (ibid.: 127)

- Of course there is no such thing as absolute and universal neutrality, it is merely a temptation.

  (Lecoq 2000: 20)

The observations about neutrality and the neutral mask in the box above are among many that could have been presented here to illustrate the breadth and variety of meanings attached to this work. While the neutral mask is perhaps the area of Lecoq's teaching most commented upon, it is – arguably – the most philosophically complex and controversial element within the school's curriculum. Lecoq says that the neutral mask, along with its antithesis, the clown, frames the student's journey through the school. The former is tackled in the first year, the latter during the second. He is unambiguous about its importance within the curriculum: 'such fundamental things occur with this mask that it has become the central point of my teaching method' (2000: 36). As professional actors, students will not wear the neutral mask again, for it is a teaching tool and not designed for performance. As suggested earlier, Lecoq developed his research and teaching on the neutral mask from Jacques Copeau – who called it the 'noble mask' – and together their work represents the most significant investigation into this teaching tool within the twentieth century.

Lecoq provides a detailed account of how he uses the neutral mask with first-year students in *The Moving Body*. Before considering the implications of this work, it may be useful to offer a summary of his approach. Unlike expressive or *commedia* masks, a well-crafted neutral mask is in a state of calm, or rest. It possesses no psychological or biographical characteristics, but is neither 'dead' nor lifeless (Figure 2.3). Ultimately, the neutral mask is a tool towards characterisation, but in the process of working with it successfully the student will acquire a range of attitudes, physical dispositions and skills appropriate to any kind of performing. With every new cohort of students Lecoq developed and continued to refine a range of incremental exercises through which he led his students. Wearing the neutral mask encourages students to find a pure economy of movement which is uncluttered by extraneous social patterns or habits, and which invites them to explore a sensual and physical relationship with the world and its matter. A relationship that is – as far as possible – untainted and uninformed by knowledge, emotion, anticipation or experience. Although the neutral mask is not a mask for performing, any observer of these exercises will have their attention directed towards the whole body of the wearer, now that the overly expressive qualities of the face are erased and rendered 'neutral'. Later, when the neutral mask is discarded in actual performance, the

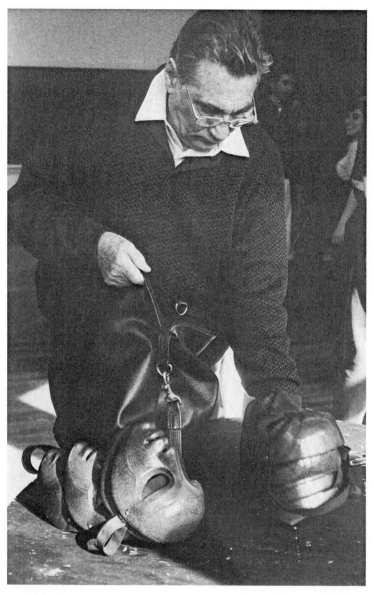

Figure 2.3 Jacques Lecoq with neutral masks. Master class for the Theatre of Creation, Lehigh University, USA (1994)

supposition is that this total body awareness will serve the actor well when tackling different forms of characterisation.

From the first exercise, entitled 'waking up', the pupil is placed in a variety of situations where he or she is invited to respond with an alive and alert neutrality – a kind of 'innocence' where the student experiences the world as if for the first time. From here follow encounters with different elements, materials and colours, leading to the discovery of animals, birds and insects. The natural world is explored in much of its diversity. Through all this it is not a question of imitation and mimicry, but of 'becoming' or 'being' the animal or material in question. Here, the student is required to *essentialise* the rhythms, patterns and textures of, for example, rubber, steel, glue, earth, air, a snake, an eagle, a tiger or a bee. Finally, this work is taken back into the dramatic dimension and now the objective is to render fire or water, vulture or chicken, cat or kangaroo 'human', so as to discover a highly physical characterisation with equally expressive vocal qualities. Lecoq calls this stage *theatrical transposition*, and it is the ultimate justification of all that has gone before in the slow and meticulous development of neutral mask work.

The landscape of neutrality thus contains a number of noteworthy features and assumptions that take us to the root of Lecoq's pedagogy. Although few other theatre teachers employ neutrality in the same way as Lecoq, there are significant propositions embedded here which are common to other forms of actor training. What follows are some of the key suppositions and characteristics in the neutral mask and associated exercises:

- Importance of stripping away – of shedding – superfluous habits and mannerisms.
- Student actor as potential *tabula rasa* – a blank sheet or empty vessel.
- Learning as a sensory and somatic experience: knowledge accrued through movement.
- The expressive potential of the whole body, not merely face, hands, etc.
- Importance of simplicity prior to layering, elaboration and complexity.
- Freeing and organising the body for economic and uncluttered movement.

•   An acceptance of concepts such as 'the truth', 'the real' and 'the artificial'.

Any investigation into the actor's quest for a state of neutrality takes us to the heart of the nature of acting. What is it to *represent*? What does *presence* mean? What is the relationship between an actor's own identity and the role he or she is playing? How far is it possible – and ethically desirable – to strip away the actor's outer shell of socialised habits and thoughts? Although there is no space here for such an enquiry, the search for neutrality also takes us – laterally – towards questions about the nature of human identity and personality.

Essentially, the neutral mask is a tool to help students approach the world sensually and somatically in the belief that such a route encourages a clearer – purer – form of knowledge than that acquired through the intellect and the cerebral faculties. In order to relate to the world in this way, it is necessary to try to place students in a state of 'unknowing' – to take them back to a condition where they only *know* the world through gesture, movement and touch, all of which, in Lecoq's analysis, originally preceded the word:

> Gesture precedes knowledge
> Gesture precedes thought
> Gesture precedes language
>   (Felner 1985: 150)

Contrary to certain tendencies within contemporary cultural and philosophical analysis which argue that we only know – and construct – the world through language, Lecoq believes that an ability to create language emerges from our need to move in order to survive. Hence, as Felner articulates it, knowledge, thought and language are all consequent upon movement and gesture. This analysis takes us as much into Lecoq's understanding of mime – and its function in society – as it does to the neutral mask. Nonetheless, it is important to understand that this philosophical position underpins all his work on neutrality.

To return to the actor's task. Work with the neutral mask assumes that acting is a physical and athletic activity as much as it is about communication through the spoken word. To acquire an expressive body, the student has first to simplify and economise movement before elaboration and complex physical characterisation can be considered. As Elderidge and Huston remark, the neutral mask is primarily 'a tool for analysing the quality of the body's action' (1995: 127). At this level, most who have used the neutral mask for teaching, and who have learned from it as students, would attest to its great value in developing an awareness of one's own body and its movement, and as a tool – or corporeal strategy – towards preparing the actor for characterisation. For theatre teachers who work with the neutral mask, it is an immensely useful device, regardless of what it might imply philosophically about identity and our being in the world.

The philosophy underlying the neutral mask can assume controversial proportions when the quest for neutrality is tackled in a literal or absolute way. If understood and pursued literally this becomes difficult territory. Here, a questionable universalism replaces a perspective which argues that bodies are sites inscribed by history, cultural context, personal biography and individual disposition. To attempt to erase these traces, so the argument goes, is not only ethically and ideologically undesirable, but ultimately impossible. The quest for neutrality becomes an attempt to strip subjects of their history and cultural identity in the name of a spurious universalism. Linked to this argument is the view that, to search for a neutral body is to obscure or erase difference. To deny difference is not to promote a common humanism, but rather to prioritise the importance of certain human qualities or characteristics at the expense of others.

Performance dramaturg and teacher John Keefe has some different reservations. Keefe, while certainly finding the term 'neutrality' and its quest with theatre students on the studio floor a very useful heuristic device, has major concerns over the philosophical implications of the concept. For Keefe, terms like neutrality, 'innocent curiosity' and 'childlike state', which are often yoked together within the journey of the neutral mask, are dangerously romantic formulations. Keefe puts it like this:

> Although I think Lecoq's understanding of the term 'neutral' is insightful and inspiring, there's sometimes an implication of trying to reach a state of pre-conscious innocence. There's a kind of dualism here – not a Cartesian one – but another kind that is almost to do with 'experience versus innocence'. There's a dualism of the conscious cluttered adult world versus a pre-conscious innocence. . . . Once we become an adult we can't turn off our consciousness. If we do we are in an Artaudian state of trance or meditation.
>
> (Keefe 2002)

Keefe's reservations are clearly important and would be articulated by a number of theatre practitioners who might have considerable respect for other aspects of Lecoq's work. However, whether Keefe's charges are fairly laid at Lecoq's door is open to debate. They are possibly more appropriate when applied to the work of Jerzy Grotowski, Eugenio Barba and, perhaps, even Peter Brook. As one reads *The Moving Body* or *Le Théâtre du geste*, there are times when Lecoq clearly seems to fall prey to Keefe's *romanticism*, but then, as the quotation below implies, he defuses such criticism by admitting that neutrality is actually – after all – a 'temptation'.

Essentially, for Lecoq the neutral mask is at once a metaphor and a practical strategy within a whole repertoire of activities designed to prepare the actor for a creative input into the process of making theatre. It is not an injunction – moral or ideological – as to how one should be in the world, or behave towards others. At root, success with the neutral mask leads to the *disponible* student – an actor who is perpetually open and in a state of discovery. As with other areas of his thinking and teaching, there is an element of playfulness and paradox in his passionate curiosity for the neutral mask. He eschews rigidity and places the self-realisation of each student at the centre of the process:

> Starting from an accepted reference point, which is neutral, the students discover their own point of view. Of course, there is no such thing as absolute and universal neutrality, it is merely a temptation.

> (Lecoq 2000: 20)

MIME AND MOVEMENT

Lecoq's relationship to mime was a complex, interesting and difficult one. Like many other artists working in the last few decades of the twentieth century, Lecoq had an uneasy relationship with *mime* as both term and concept. He changed the name of his school at least four times, and on each occasion altered the relationship of the 'M' word to others in the title. Today – and since the 1990s – *mime* has been dropped altogether, and the institution is simply called 'International Theatre School' (École Internationale de Théâtre). Still, however, in some quarters the first reaction to hearing Lecoq's name is that he ran a 'mime school'. Although, as we shall see, Lecoq was always at great pains to distinguish his teaching and theorising from the practice of Marcel Marceau – and from Marceau's teacher, Étienne Decroux – he never embraced any of the fashionable synonyms for mime such as 'physical theatre' or 'visual performance'. Instead, Lecoq continued throughout his life to attempt to wrest the meaning and practice of mime away from white-faced illusion – those imaginary glass walls – towards something more subtle, profound and ultimately crucial to the realisation of effective theatre.

In Myra Felner's comprehensive and analytical account of twentieth-century French mime – *The Apostles of Silence* (1985) – she examines in considerable depth the finer distinctions that Lecoq makes about mime, its origin, its rediscovery through Copeau and Decroux and its currency for contemporary theatre. In particular, she notes and identifies some crucial distinctions between Decroux's theory and practice and that of Lecoq. In the account that follows I make no attempt to retrace Felner's engaging and detailed analysis, but rather to map the main features of how Lecoq uses and understands mime through his own writing and teaching.

In *The Moving Body* Lecoq apparently writes little on mime, and in his school he did not teach it, or at least did not teach it as a technique to be distinguished from other forms of movement preparation and skill acquisition. Confusingly, he also uses the terms *mimage*, *mimisme* and *mimodynamic*, which translator, David Bradby, explains in the book's glossary. Moreover, Lecoq distinguishes between *action mime*, *cartoon mime*, *figurative mime*, *melomime*, *open mime* and *storytelling mime*, devoting only very short passages to each in the book. For the reader of *The Moving Body*, expecting to discover how Lecoq taught and conceptualised mime, this is indeed puzzling. And yet Lecoq's understanding of mime permeates the whole book and is, of course, central to what he believed the creative actor should be doing for the 'new theatre for tomorrow'. It is in *Le Théâtre du geste* (1987) – subtitled *Mimes et acteurs* – however, that we can find a far more extensive investigation into what constituted mime.

Lecoq distinguishes his 'open mime' from pantomime on the one hand and mere imitation or mimicry on the other. Like the circus clown, the *pantomime* mime has little to offer theatre. Under the heading of gestural languages, pantomime – along with figurative, cartoon and storytelling mime – makes a brief appearance at the school in the beginning of the second year. Lecoq is not interested in these forms in their own right, but as a 'sort of warm-up before we plunge into the dramatic territories to come. It is important not to see the technical dimension

On mime – Lecoq, Jousse and Dr Hacks

• To mime is a fundamental action, the foundation of dramatic creation, not only for the actor, but also for writing and for performance. For me, mime is central to theatre.

(Lecoq 2000: 21)

• Children mime the world in order to get to know it and to prepare themselves to live in it. Theatre is a game which merely extends this action in different ways.

(ibid.: 22)

• To mime is literally to embody and therefore to understand better . . . miming is a way of rediscovering a thing with renewed freshness. The action of miming becomes a form of knowledge.

(ibid.)

• Every true artist is a mime. Picasso's ability to draw a bull depended on his having found the *essential* bull in himself, which released the shaping gesture of his hand. He was miming. Painters and sculptors are outstanding mime artists because they share in the same act of embodiment.

(ibid.)

• The mime which I love involves an identification with things in order to make them live, even when words are used.

(ibid.)

of the different languages as an end in itself, but to enrich it continuously with dramatic states' (Lecoq 2000: 104). (See Figures 2.4, 2.5 and 2.6.)

Mime, simply as imitation, mimicry or mimesis, holds little consequence for Lecoq. Here, he finds the conventional wisdom, which sees mime as a language of gestures to *replace* the spoken word, misleading and restrictive. 'One visualises an actor who does not speak, and who uses stylised gestures to show objects which do not exist, or makes faces to indicate that he laughs or cries. In this sense . . . we don't do mime

- Mime differentiates itself from mimicry in that it is not merely an imitation, but a grasp of the reality which is part of our lives. . . . Man thinks with his whole being. . . . There is not only a thinking head, but a whole human which learns and mimes using his entire body.

  (Jousse, cited in Lecoq 1987: 17)

- The true mime exists in the depths of silence where gesture does not replace speech.

  (Lecoq 1987: 96)

- Lecoq believes that Beckett is the greatest author of the modern mime, because he understands the true nature of the clown.

  (Felner 1985: 166)

- Mime is the very essence of all living theatre . . . [it] has shaken itself loose from the formalism by which it was previously bound. And this has revealed several possibilities for the journey towards the theatre of gesture, images and the spoken word.

  (Brochure advertising a Lecoq summer school)

- In his book 'Le Geste', Dr Hacks, who himself was a mime, tells us: 'a good mime must be 1.7 metres tall, must have strong muscles, a thoracic circumference of 91 centimetres, the ability to lift 95 kilos, a dorsal resistance of 29 kilos, a spring of 44 centimetres and at least 36 centimetres of circumference in the arms. His weight must not be over 60 kilos and 700 grams.' . . . Too bad for the others!

  (Lecoq 1987: 56)

– not that kind of mime' (Lecoq 1973: 117). More acerbically, he notes that many contemporary mimes:

> express themselves in a way far removed from silence, via gesticulating as though crying for help or pulling a face in order to remedy a lack of speech and to make themselves understood. These poor mimes have caused the genre to be viewed as a strange zoological phenomenon which one should observe from behind a glass screen – a kind of theatrical malady.
>
> (Lecoq 1987: 96)

Figure 2.4
Company
Lecoq (1959)

Figure 2.5
(left)
I speak
and I move,
Schiller
Theatre,
Berlin
(1963)

Figure 2.6
(right)
The punter,
Schiller
Theatre,
Berlin
(1963)

I am also reminded here of Philippe Gaulier – 'moi, je déteste le mime' – who, when despairing of some overly cute characterisation from a student, would offer a critique that the unfortunate individual was playing like a 'tubercular little mime artist'. Behind the humour, both men are making a more serious point. For Lecoq, mime as mimicry and as a stylised language of gesture, however skilful, is of limited value for theatre, largely because it closes down creative choices for the actor. This 'silent formalism', or what David Bradby describes in a footnote as 'a representation of form' (Lecoq 2000: 22), runs counter to almost everything the school seems to stand for. If, for Lecoq, making successful theatre was about harnessing the dynamic qualities of play, improvisation, curiosity, risk, voice and movement to serve the dramatic territory in question, then a system of codified mime offers little to this task. In *Le Théâtre du geste*, Lecoq identifies a defining moment in his life when he distilled his views on mime as 'silent formalism'. He tells the story of arriving in Padua in 1948 and proudly giving a demonstration of the famous 'walking on the spot', which had been invented by Decroux and Barrault. After he had finished, one of the actors, Agostino Cantorello, stood up and said:

> 'Che Bello! Che Bello! Ma dove va?' (*It's good! It's good! But where are you going?*) This phrase stayed with me like a symbol of the heightened awareness I felt for mime from then on: I understood that mime which stands isolated and alone is going nowhere.
>
> (Lecoq 1987: 109)

It is here that a chasm of aspiration between Lecoq and Decroux is opened up. Decroux devoted his life, which ended tragically in extreme poverty, to researching and constructing a codified language and grammar designed to provide mime with an aesthetic and formal rigour that would enable it to stand alone as an art form – distinct from theatre on one side and from dance on the other. Ironically, the technique behind the popular mime of Marceau and his countless disciples is predicated upon Decroux's *grammaire*, the result of fifty years of dedicated research and teaching. Decroux trained Marceau, but was ultimately disdainful of the popular form of mime produced by his illustrious pupil. Notwithstanding the mutual hostility between some of the disciples of both men, Lecoq and Decroux had an amicable – if distant – relationship. In *Le Théâtre du geste*, Lecoq admits to 'respecting'

Decroux, and Fay Lecoq recalls him ringing one day to ask if her husband – the trained physiotherapist – would help his son, Maximilian, who was having back problems at the time.

Lecoq regarded Decroux's system as 'severe' and – by implication – unconnected to 'life', overly formal and one which 'locked shut' the creative potential of the actor. Nonetheless, a close reading of each man's analysis of movement reveals areas of similarity and overlap. Both analysed, for example, stillness and silence, affirmed the importance of the fixed point, explored the principles of equilibrium, and identified pulling and pushing as the two essential human actions. The difference, however, is that, while for Decroux this detailed analysis of movement was to lead ultimately to an ambitious and codified system – the deep structure upon which mime as an autonomous art form would be based – for Lecoq the quest was to uncover those dynamic motors of movement and gesture which would enable the student to harness the rhythms and spirit of 'life' to the task of acting. For Lecoq, detailed technical work on movement was a useful discipline for the student, but ultimately only the means to a more important *dramatic* end.

In this process of studying movement technique, Lecoq's overriding concern was to discover the forces and patterns of movement which underpin both particular emotional states – the dynamics of fatigue and nostalgia, for example – and the main dramatic territories which will be investigated by students during their second year at the school. Here, Lecoq squares the circle between his analysis of movement and gesture with an overriding focus upon the dynamics of space. When describing the school's work on movement technique, he summarises his hypothesis and indicates an approach to teaching:

> Vertical movement situates man between heaven and earth, between zenith and nadir, in a tragic event. Tragedy is always vertical: the gods are on Mount Olympus. *Bouffons* are also vertical, but in the other direction: their gods are underground. As for the diagonal it is sentimental, it flies off and we cannot tell where it will come down. This is the terrain of the broad emotions of melodrama.
>
> Every dramatic territory can be assigned its precise spatial situation and the physical movements we study, from the simplest to the most complex, take their place in these dramatic dimensions. I love. I pull. I hate. I push.

> (Lecoq 2000: 83)

For Lecoq, therefore, the study of mime is central to the school's curriculum, but paradoxically, nowhere is it taught as such. 'To mime is to embody and therefore to understand better' writes Lecoq in *The Moving Body*. This is central to his philosophy of teaching theatre. One might say that the actor, whose task is to capture and translate the rhythms of life, cannot fully understand the world without attempting to embody it. So, although physical skill and discipline are required to learn mime, that in itself is of secondary importance to a deep knowledge of the material world which comes from this activity – mime – as Lecoq defined it. This position firmly places Lecoq among those who reject the philosophy of Descartes where, as we have already seen, mind and body are separate, the latter functioning at the behest of a directing mind. In *Le Théâtre du geste*, Lecoq writes:

> To consider the human body as an instrument has always been to take a rather simplistic view. There has often been a tendency to view it like a keyboard, under the influence of the hands which play it to bring out the possibilities of the instrument and to call up virtuoso performances. The true mime reaches into the kingdom of Movement (with a capital M) and does not confuse exercise with style.

(Lecoq 1987: 95)

MAKING SPACE: LABORATORY FOR THE STUDY OF MOVEMENT (LEM)

A strikingly designed leaflet folding out to a poster advertises LEM. On one side a black and white photograph reveals a workshop cluttered with apparently unfinished, gravity-defying wood or cardboard models that reach towards, or are suspended from, the ceiling. In one corner a figure standing on a bench stretches to secure a structure; elsewhere discarded boxes, balsa wood, corrugated cardboard and staple and glue guns mingle to create a contrasting sense of order and creative chaos. In the models, curves and angles compete to produce shapes that are at once abstract, human and – sometimes – animal. This is not a gallery, more a messy, alive and unfinished space where much has to be completed. This is the workspace of LEM, a long narrow studio that lies immediately adjacent to the main school.

On the other side of the leaflet – black and white now discarded – eleven plates reveal carefully completed structures occasionally displaying a flash of colour in a wooden strut or cardboard panel. All seem precarious and impossibly fragile, and the more one looks the more a sense of movement vies with the stillness of each structure. Some seem to dance or twirl, while others lean, stoop or reach impossibly for the sky. Occasionally, a structure invites us to offer interpretation or meaning, but all possess a movement dynamic that directs the gaze, tightens the belly, drops the shoulders, opens the fingers, turns the head or tilts the trunk fractionally to left or right, forward or back – a Cubist delight. Beneath the panels is a quote from J. Lecoq:

The blown up body (Le corps éclaté)

A standing body, reduced to an axial stick
(gauge), holds in its different parts,
preferential colours in the analogy of their
space (colours-body).
From this gauge the blown up body is built, in
a dynamic language, embodying, space,
rhythm, and force.

To the side of these plates, replicated in French and English, is a description of LEM: the body and space, the body and movement, feelings and colours. Now it is taught by Pascale Lecoq and Krikor Belekian – both architects and set designers. Pascale is Lecoq's daughter; Krikor has jointly taught the course for nearly thirty years, first with Lecoq and now with his daughter, familial continuity helping to construct an understanding of space. Currently, LEM runs for one year on three evenings a week during term time. Some participants will be first-year students from the two-year theatre course, but many are from outside, such as architects, visual artists, scenographers, actors and directors – usually a disparate group, united only by their interest in the relationship between bodies, movement, materials and space (Figure 2.7).

LEM was introduced to the school in 1976 and, according to Pascale Lecoq, it has changed and developed considerably since then. In a conversation with the author, Pascale summarised what LEM was about:

The end product of LEM is a plastic performance – people moving themselves with objects in the space. Students are coming to the course to find the

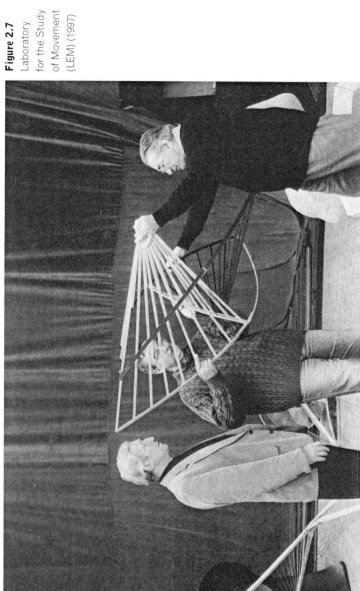

Figure 2.7
Laboratory
for the Study
of Movement
(LEM) (1997)

relationship between the body and space. They discover things with their body and afterwards they translate these discoveries into drawing or construction. It's really a process – like the school – a voyage. Today, it's more about scenography.

(Pascale Lecoq 2001)

Essentially, the conceptual assumptions that underpin LEM are these:

- We can only fully understand human movement by considering its impact on space. Movement displaces and reorganises the space around it.
- The form, purpose and organisation of space have a profound impact on how we move in it. We move differently in a supermarket and a church, a bedroom and a kitchen, a gymnasium and a railway station, a broad boulevard and a country lane, a pavement café and a grand hotel.
- Human passions and emotions – and also colours – have spatial qualities and consequences.
- The dominant passions in different dramatic territories – tragedy, melodrama or farce, for example – will inform the scenographic principles for each of these genres of theatre.
- Sensitivity towards space is crucial for the creative actor.

In practice, the LEM student will experience two main interlocking strands within the course: movement work which engages and brings into play the miming body and, second, creative work that entails the building – and subsequent 'animation' – of structures which seek to capture, express and bring to life the qualities of the movements explored hitherto. Paradoxically, LEM works both at a considerable level of conceptual abstraction, but also practically as students construct and engineer models in space.

The final part of the course requires the students to work from the external stimulation of a piece of music or poetry, a sculpture or a story, a memory or a landscape. Upon such provocations students build portable structures – from wood, string, cardboard, etc. From this point they will seek to discover how these structures move in space, always avoiding illustration, anecdote and literalness. Finally, they will 'perform' these constructions in front of an invited audience. Here the task is to identify the essential movement dynamic of the structure that in turn has emerged organically from the original thematic impulse. For the drama student the experience provides a taste of the principles entailed in theatre scenography – not in any detailed or literal manner, but to identify the underlying codes, values and *motors* embedded in a particular theatrical form. Lecoq gives an example:

> Taking *Hamlet* as a theme would obviously not involve learning how to construct the set for the first act, but rather showing the future scenographer how spaces must be constructed which *await* the drama to be played out. When he inscribes in space the scenography of *Hamlet*, the space itself will hold the density of the drama.
>
> (Lecoq 2000: 156)

For architects, however, LEM is a reminder – or an invitation to take note – that, in the buildings they design, there will be bodies moving within the constituent spaces. To understand something about the dynamics of human movement, and how such movement is altered and shaped by different spaces, is crucial – so argue the teachers of LEM – for the successful realisation of an architect's design. Pascale Lecoq puts this point rather more poetically:

> Sometimes both architects and theatre students only think about space from the head. For us, the more important thing is that you think with your whole body. The work we are doing with our students does not suggest that you should forget your head, but rather that you should try to put all your sensations into your body. For architects too: before you build a house, fill it with your body and not simply with your head.
>
> (2001)

LEM presents us with some of the most enigmatic and elusive elements of Lecoq's work. Clearly, its subject material lay at the centre of his curiosity and unquenchable desire to investigate form, matter and movement. It was palpably Lecoq's *laboratory*, and parallels with the process of scientific research are not difficult to discern. The 'discoveries' made in LEM by Lecoq with generations of students fed his imagination for teaching next door. While LEM seems curiously separate from the school's daily routines, it is clear that the work here provoked ideas and reflection on the development of his teaching on the two-year course. And yet Lecoq devotes barely more than two pages to LEM in *The Moving Body*, concluding with an almost terse remark that 'The experience of the LEM course is very practical and no written explanation could do it justice. It brings each student face to face with himself' (Lecoq 2000: 157). For those LEM students who were also at the school, there was no expectation that they should try to utilise their experiments within a theatrical context. Indeed, Lecoq actively discouraged any attempt to transpose LEM experiments directly into performance.

So the paradox of LEM is that, while the lived experience of actually doing the course is immensely practical and somatic – it is not about abstract theorising on the subject of space, it seems to defy any attempt to capture its meaning clearly and explicitly through the written word. Perhaps too, given that Lecoq imprinted such a personal stamp on this aspect of the school's work, he was unwilling to talk and write about it at any great length. Echoing Pascale Lecoq's comment below, Andy Crook suggests that LEM represented the most original and radical elements of Lecoq's entire body of work:

> I think where his heart really lay was in architecture and design. In those areas I felt he was much more 'cutting edge'. I always felt that this was his *heartbeat*, as it were. I think in a way he was only doing what we do when we work in performance art, and it was an experiment. He was just fascinated by form and shape – about space and time.
>
> (Crook 2002)

Certainly LEM suggests connections to particular forms of live art practice, to the process and work of Polish artist and theatre director, Tadeusz Kantor, for example, and – in Lecoq's willingness to use the term *laboratory* – with Peter Brook (Figure 2.8) and Jerzy Grotowski. Today, Pascale Lecoq and Krikor Belekian carry the torch for LEM as strongly as ever, and it was to be extended to two years from the autumn of 2002. At this point Jos Houben, who teaches on the theatre course, and other guest tutors joined Pascale and Krikor to form an enlarged team devoted to deepening this very particular dimension of the school's work. Pascale is absolutely clear about how important this area of work was to her father: 'at the end of his life my father's dream was to write a book about LEM. Towards the end, it was the foundation of the school – the essence of the school' (Pascale Lecoq 2001).

Figure 2.8
Peter Brook
and Jacques
Lecoq (1973)

END WORDS

From an examination of Lecoq's writing and spoken words, this chapter has attempted to identify and explore the main principles behind his work. I have done this by considering *how* he taught at the school, and *what* the main areas of substance were in the – changing – curriculum. There has been no attempt to describe each subject area described in *The Moving Body*, for to have done so would have been to replicate whole areas of his writing for no useful purpose. In Chapter 5, I consider several of the main issues in Lecoq's life and work which deserve further investigation, and offer some initial thoughts on his contribution to late twentieth-century Western theatre.

3

TRACES OF
JACQUES LECOQ

Théâtre de Complicité's
Street of Crocodiles and the
work of Mummenschanz

For most of the titles that figure in the Performance Practitioners series, this chapter will focus on one production directed by the theatre practitioner in question. Although Lecoq certainly directed professionally when working in Italy between 1948 and 1956, and did so again sporadically in Europe for television, film and the stage up until the 1980s, there is little documented evidence from which to study such work. More importantly, however, it would seem strange to focus on Lecoq as *director* when the overwhelming thrust of this account has been to consider his contribution to world theatre as teacher and theorist of actor training.

Here, I direct my attention towards tracing Lecoq's influence through the work of two very different companies, most of whose founder members trained at his Paris school. As Franc Chamberlain explains in *Jacques Lecoq and the British Theatre*, detecting his influence upon the theatre of Britain, or indeed any country, is a difficult and risk-laden task. Chamberlain observes:

> There is no ensemble with whom Lecoq is uniquely associated, no performer who is the Lecoq disciple *par excellence*. Lecoq offers a method of working, what the students do with it is up to them. He does not direct them. He does not tell them what to say. . . . Lecoq's work cannot be 'diluted'

or 'polluted' by graduates developing it in their own way; there is no pure
Lecoq form.

(Chamberlain and Yarrow 2002: 4)

The risks in examining the work of two companies in order to
identify the traces of Lecoq's teaching are several. First, there is the
danger of reducing a complex relationship to a crudely mechanical and
deterministic one. Second, the possibility exists of rendering a dis-
service to such companies by ignoring other influences that have shaped
their work, and the extent to which participants have forged their
own collective creative identity over the course of time. Finally, there
is the hazard of imposing a stifling post-hoc academic framework
on to a relationship that is, in fact, fluid, organic and endlessly under
negotiation.

In public statements, interviews, programme notes and film credits,
both companies are ready to acknowledge Lecoq's influence and what
follows takes such willingness at its face value. The choice of Théâtre
de Complicité's director, Simon McBurney, to write a foreword to the
English translation of Lecoq's book speaks of a warm relationship
between the two men, and of a debt the former is happy to acknowledge to his old teacher. Similarly, Bernie Schürch, one of the founders
of Mummenschanz, is featured in the 1999 profile of Lecoq, *Les Deux
Voyages de Jacques Lecoq*, shown on French television. Here, Schürch talks
of Lecoq opening up their preconceptions of mask work, and of his
encouragement 'to go towards the unreasonable, to go beyond the
conceivable' (Roy and Carasso 1999).

However, it is twenty years since the founder members of
Complicité trained with Lecoq and over thirty since Bernie Schürch and
Andres Bossard of Mummenschanz left the Paris school. During the
intervening period, the possibilities for these artists to revise, reject,
forget, embellish, distort and reconstruct the principles and practices
of what they learned with Lecoq are considerable. Moreover, the desir-
ability of any mature artist seeking renewal and change through
alternative sources of influence and inspiration over such a time can
neither be denied nor disparaged. The purpose, therefore, of this
account is not to construct a rigid framework which identifies in the
work of Mummenschanz and Complicité a Lecoq injunction here, or a
specific teaching exercise there – a checklist of Lecoq precepts which
when found to be present in the work of these two companies 'proves

the case' of his influence and legacy. To frame the task in this way would be to diminish and fundamentally misunderstand what his teaching represented. Rather, it is to scan this work, so as to trace where the spirit of Lecoq – his principles, passions, preoccupations, discoveries, insights, prejudices and idiosyncrasies – apparently live on and are being reinvented or discovered afresh by those who once trained with him.

THE CASE OF THÉÂTRE DE COMPLICITÉ

Théâtre de Complicité was launched in 1982 by Simon McBurney, Marcello Magni and Annabel Arden. Magni and McBurney had met at Lecoq's school in 1980 and McBurney and Arden had been students together at Cambridge. For much of the 1980s, Complicité made comic-devised work and, like many young companies, toured extensively on the small-scale theatre circuit, initially in Britain, but increasingly throughout Europe. While the founding trio had imagined they might locate themselves in France, it was, in fact, London where the company established its base. Complicité has always operated as a loose international ensemble of performers, designers, administrators and musicians. However, what unites most of the actors who have performed with the company is that they have either trained with Lecoq, or undertaken a variety of workshops with Philippe Gaulier and Monika Pagneux. Hence, most Complicité performers have been exposed – with varying degrees of immersion – to a common lexicon of precepts and practices from these three renowned teachers of theatre, movement and acting. Complicité actors can therefore draw upon a shared basic *vocabulary* when tackling any new theatre project. At the centre of this lies, one imagines, a rooted belief and confidence that the actor's job is a creative one in the plural authorship of the piece in question, and not merely one of interpretation.

Throughout much of the 1980s Théâtre de Complicité's work was devised from the ideas, preoccupations and passions of the ensemble. Confidence bred from Lecoq's weekly *auto-cours* fed the company's founder members with a belief that, rather than having to rely on existing play scripts, they could collectively create their own texts for theatre – a tendency shared with many other small companies emerging from the Paris school. Almost all of Complicité's early work was comic, though often bleakly and mordantly so. Preoccupation with the tragic has rarely been far from the narratives constructed by the company.

A Minute Too Late (1984) was inspired by funeral parlours, a cemetery and the death of McBurney's father; *More Bigger Snacks Now* (1985) featured four men on a grimy sofa fantasising about friendship and consumerism; *Please, Please, Please* (1986) revealed the wreckage of a family Christmas; and *Anything for a Quiet Life* (1988) chillingly explored the banalities and submerged hysteria of office life. It is less well known that, during this period, the company not only created a number of solo shows with Tim Barlow, Linda Kerr Scott and Celia Gore Booth, but also experimented in music theatre with *Miss Donnithorne's Maggot*, *Escape for Tuba* and *The Phantom Violin*.

Conventional wisdom sometimes suggests that, after six or seven years, Complicité finally 'grew up and got serious', abandoned devising comedy and started doing 'significant' plays. This change of direction was either to be deplored or celebrated according to one's disposition. Reality, of course, was more complex and such accounts gloss over the tragic dimension of much of the company's early work, and ignore the inventive devising qualities that were later applied to plays (*The Winter's Tale*, *The Visit* and *The Caucasian Chalk Circle*) and stories adapted for the stage (*Out of a House Walked a Man . . .* , *Street of Crocodiles* and *The Three Lives of Lucy Cabrol*). With *Mnemonic* (1999) the company has apparently returned again to the devising process. However, to suggest that the categories of devised work, play script and adapted story are each mutually exclusive, demanding totally different approaches to theatre making, is fundamentally to misunderstand the way Complicité works. Regardless of a project's starting point, the company harnesses the same commitment to the visual and corporeal dimensions of performance, and an inventive and collaborative approach to authorship. This much remains constant.

THE STREET OF CROCODILES

Having seen many of Complicité's productions since the mid-1980s, I had – in theory – a wide range of choices upon which to construct this case study. I have chosen *The Street of Crocodiles* (hereafter merely *Crocodiles*), because it seemed the best exemplar of Complicité's work from the late 1980s through the 1990s for this particular purpose. Rehearsed and premiered in partnership with London's National Theatre in 1991, and based upon the short stories of Polish writer, Bruno Schulz (1892–1942), *Crocodiles* was relatively early in the company's exploration of the theatrical large-scale, following critical affirmation it had received for the production of Dürrenmatt's play, *The Visit*. Writing in the preface to the script for *Crocodiles* published in 1999, Simon McBurney and Mark Wheatley noted that 'eight years after the journey began, it is still migrating, developing and changing' (Théâtre de Complicité 1999).

On and off for over eight years *Crocodiles* toured the world, receiving awards and accolades. I saw the production early in its history at Edinburgh's Traverse Theatre and, by chance, on a day that marked the fiftieth anniversary of the Nazi's destruction of the Warsaw ghetto. This coincidence added an extra degree of poignancy to what was already a highly emotionally charged piece of theatre. In the account that follows, I shall devote relatively little space to describing or analysing *Crocodiles* as such. Rather, my concern here is to identify those qualities within the piece that seem to articulate and resonate with some of the key principles embodied in Lecoq's teaching. As well as considering the company's strategies in rehearsal, I shall look at a number of the dramaturgical devices employed in the piece – for example, the *life* of material objects, the physicalising of text and the harnessing of individual performers into an ensemble. In addition, I want to propose that there is an intriguing congruence between some of Lecoq's own preoccupations and Complicité's choice of Schulz's stories as the driving impulse behind this particular production.

PRETTY MUCH BORN FOR EACH OTHER: SCHULZ AND COMPLICITÉ

Complicité's production draws upon two collections of Schulz's stories: *The Street of Crocodiles* (1934) and *Sanatorium Under the Sign of the Hourglass* (1937). The stories, although fantastical and dreamlike – or nightmarish – seem to capture an extraordinary level of detail about human foibles in small-town Poland between the wars. Often peopled by members of his own family, Schulz's fictions are at times closely biographical, although never in a literal manner. Madness, ill health and eroticism thread their way through the narratives, coexisting with bizarrely sumptuous descriptions of matter and animal life. The writing is deeply sensual; at one moment conveying the scents of a hazy summer's afternoon, at another, the emotional anguish of loneliness born from an inability to make real contact with other human beings,

Schultz and Complicité

- Schulz and Théâtre de Complicité are pretty much born for each other, because there is a complete inter-connectedness of character, object, music, sound, image . . . it's completely illogical and it's desperately searching for some sort of poetry.

  (Théâtre de Complicité [Annabel Arden] 1992)

- The Complicité players are natural Schulz interpreters. Like him they transmogrify life, grotesquely changing forms and appearances . . . they see visual reality as unstable, the way Schulz sees narrative reality.

  (Fulford 1988)

- [Théâtre de Complicité] is attracted to the marginalized and the dispossessed, and takes them into the centre: the writings of the Polish Jew, Bruno Schulz, snuffed out by the Holocaust, in *The Street of Crocodiles*, say.

  (Gardner 1997)

- Schulz's writing provides no obvious key to dramatisation. It embodies the elastic, unmanageable and adhesive qualities of time. . . . There is little dialogue, no enticing narrative in the ordinary sense and not a hint of the conventional satisfactions of dramatic structure.

  (McBurney 1992)

especially women. Schulz writes of a material world constantly in a state of flux and instability, where boredom is the main driving force of curiosity, and where joy of the erotic is to be derived from punishment and guilt. Schulz's writing has been compared to Proust ('inflation of the past and ecstatic reaches of simile') and Kafka ('father obsession and metamorphic fantasies') (Updike 1988: 118).

Like all Complicité's work, *Crocodiles* was never 'finished' and, perhaps, experienced more revisions over eight years than many of the company's other productions. The piece of theatre I witnessed in Edinburgh in the early 1990s would have looked different in significant ways to a performance of *Crocodiles* I might have seen at London's

Queen's Theatre during January 1999. Making little attempt either to communicate Schulz's life in any chronological sequence, or to retell his tales, Complicité's *Crocodiles* jettisons the normal rules of linear narrative, placing elements, themes and curious details from the stories within a larger personal and historical frame. Through selected fragments of Schulz's fiction, we begin to construct a picture of his life and the times in which he lived. The outer frame of the drama exposes the personal tragedy of Schulz's life – shot by a Gestapo officer in the Drohobycz ghetto in November 1942. But this in turn is placed within the larger picture of central European history during the 1920s and 1930s, culminating in the rise of Nazi Germany and the ensuing Holocaust and World War. In notes at the beginning of the script's 1999 publication, McBurney and Wheatley convey something of how the company worked in creating *Crocodiles*:

> Our process involved not only the writing of original dialogue (as with any play) but also the lifting of text direct from the stories (and from Schulz's letters and essays). We used descriptions of him given to us by Jacob. We worked on improvisations in which the actors played out the process of memory which lies at the heart of all his stories. We created the atmosphere of his times and the mechanism of his dreams. We investigated the rhythm of his nightmares and his intense engagement with his beloved and despised solitude.
>
> (Théâtre de Complicité 1999)

Jacob Schulz was Bruno's nephew. He worked closely with the company throughout the devising process and as the work began to tour. Jacob died in 1997 and both text and the final performances of *Crocodiles* were dedicated to him.

PREPARATION, DEVISING AND REHEARSAL

One of the defining features of Lecoq's teaching was a refusal to separate physical preparation – or training – from dramatic creation. In Chapter 4 of this book a sequence of practical tasks, exercises and improvisations leading into three dramatic territories well illustrates this approach. From the BBC2 *Late Show* profile of Complicité in rehearsal for *Crocodiles*, we catch glimpses of how *stuff* – theatrical material – was created. Early in the process we watch members of the cast working in pairs, sitting back-to-back on the floor. Here, as one slowly leans backwards the other curls forward, so, like Siamese twins, their backs appear joined from pelvis to neck. Exploring their backs they stretch and push: no great physical exertion, rather a gentle discovery of each other's spines, leading into imbalances and sometimes to a position of standing – bodies opening and preparing. Now, we have a brief glimpse of actors trying out simple lifts and carries. 'We're looking for that little moment', says McBurney, 'which might get into the show' (*The Late Show* 1992). A little later, we watch director McBurney inviting the pairs to roll together 'just a couple of yards across the floor'. Developing the exercise further, two actors gently engaged in a rolling embrace are helped on their way by a third. 'Tu le pousse' ('you push him'), says the director. So far there is no obvious sense of any dramatic business in the making, but several things are happening: bodies are preparing themselves, Lecoq's basic motors of dramatic creation – pushing and pulling – are being explored, although at this stage without context or specific theatrical purpose, and all the while a slow and hidden nurturing of *complicité* and ensemble is being physically constructed among the performers.

In a moment, the camera pans across the rehearsal studio to reveal what we later recognise as the opening sequence of the show. From the clever editing of a television documentary it is impossible to know how many actual days or weeks have elapsed since the first back-to-back exercise, or indeed how close to opening night is this point in rehearsal. Nonetheless, we watch:

- Annabel Arden (The Mother) shuffling forward on her knees, carrying a huge book on her left shoulder;
- Cesar Sarachu (Joseph – the fictional representation of Schulz himself) sensually smelling and stroking a book;
- Clive Mendus (Uncle Charles) and Hayley Carmichael (Maria) locked together, rolling slowly and lyrically across the floor;
- Matthew Scurfield (The Father) walking deliberately, but lightly, across the space with Lilo Baur (The Maid) draped over his shoulders;
- Antonio Gill Martinez (Cousin Emil) searching through the pages of a book, and crossing the space with Joyce Carmichael (Agatha), similarly draped over his shoulders;
- Stefan Metz (Leon) bent double, slowly 'stepping' a pair of heavy boots, which he is holding by their heels; and

- the legs of Eric Mallett (Theodore) descending a ladder. In performance he will 'walk' down the back wall, suspended by a (concealed) rope.

As the documentary reaches its conclusion, we watch the opening few minutes of *Crocodiles* on its first night, and here the fruits of this journey from first movement exercise to fully realised dramatic material are made explicit. Of course, from the scenario detailed above there have been further revisions. Notably, actor Scurfield has replaced Mendus in the rolling sequence with Carmichael, and now, holding a book, he reads: 'once early in the morning towards the end of winter I visited such a forgotten chamber. From all the crevices in the floor, from all the mouldings, from every recess there grew slim shoots' (Théâtre de Complicité 1999: 7).

I have traced this progression of events in some detail, as in a graphic way it fleshes out a central principle of Lecoq's teaching. Apart from the precept identified above of not isolating physical preparation from dramatic creation, the sequence also illustrates another fundamental dimension of Lecoq's thinking, namely that motion provokes emotion. To put it another way, one can begin to construct characters – and the meanings for which they are a vehicle – by working physically rather than through psychological motivation. While this is not an insight unique to Lecoq (cf. Meyerhold, Grotowski and Barba), it is a critical element in his approach to theatre dramaturgy. McBurney encapsulates the devising and creative process deconstructed above:

> The structure is much more one of a cross between a sculptor and a football team where I will simply be trying to lead people from a game into an exercise – a physical exercise to build up their strength – into another game, which leads into a scene, and from out of the scene . . . so they hardly know when they are in a scene or not in a scene.
>
> (*The Late Show* 1992)

For Lecoq the term *preparation* – rather than notions of training, skills, techniques, etc. – captured the essence of his project. Of course, students acquired new skills during their time at the school, but this was almost as a by-product of something more important, namely a confidence to play imaginatively and creatively. It was also, I suggest, a confidence to be open to all creative possibilities and the corollary of this: enough personal and collective strength to admit to not knowing answers and solutions. While Lecoq's pedagogy, as we have seen, was built upon some unyielding principles, within this framework he firmly believed in the notion that uncertainty leads to discovery. For any artist, too much certainty closes shut the possibility of creative discovery. I have reiterated these points because they seem to capture the spirit of Complicité's journey through a typical rehearsal process, and particularly as they approached *Crocodiles*.

In *The Moving Body*, Lecoq writes about the 'ricochet effect', that is to say, an approach that welcomes the unexpected and the unanticipated as triggers for creative discovery. McBurney acknowledges something similar when tackling a new show:

> I often ask myself what the origin is for doing a piece and I have to conclude that there is no origin: if you start looking for a single point of departure you will never find it. ... I'll have an impulse and during rehearsals I'll go miles and miles away from it only to return to it, to revisit and refind the point of departure.

(McBurney 1999b: 67)

However, the crucial point here is that a director can only really have confidence to ride with so much uncertainty and fluidity in a rehearsal period if the ground has been prepared in advance. For Complicité, part of this 'ground preparation' has already been achieved, because almost all the actors have experienced the teaching of Lecoq, Gaulier and Pagneux at one time or another, and hence arrive at the first day of rehearsals with a 'common language'. This, says McBurney, means a 'physical, vocal, musical and architectural language: all those elements which make up a theatre language' (1999b: 75). The preparation, however, continues into rehearsal and becomes contextualised by the 'collective imagining' of the cast around the impulse or theme of the project. It is important to stress again that this preparation does not isolate the purely physical or technical from the creative. It is a linked preparation for a state of mind and for the musculature, of the individual actor and of the ensemble – none separated from the other. An approach, it is salutary to note, that is peculiar neither to Lecoq's teaching nor McBurney's directing, but one which links them laterally both to Peter Brook, on the one hand, and Joan Littlewoood, on the other, and historically back to Meyerhold and Copeau. McBurney encapsulates the process of preparation like this:

The value in preparation, other than facilitating greater communication between people, is again to do with the unexpected. I do not prepare people so that they know about where they are going. I prepare them so that they are ready: ready to change, ready to be surprised, ready to seize any opportunity that comes their way.

(1999b: 71)

THE LIFE OF MATERIAL OBJECTS

In these stories, Schulz's vision – his obsessive preoccupation – is with the existence of matter. From the stultifying boredom of daily life in Drohobycz and from the loneliness he managed both to cherish and loathe, Schulz constructed an imaginative world 'in which human beings, objects, spaces take on temporary unstable shapes and forms before metamorphosing into new ones. The accent is always on *trans-formation*' (Croft 1992). In an interview with his friend, Polish playwright Stanislaw Witkiewicz, Schulz writes that matter is:

In a state of perpetual fermentation, germination, potential life. There are no dead, hard limited objects. Everything spreads beyond its own boundaries, remains but a moment in its given shape, only to abandon it at the first opportunity.

(Schulz 1980)

Earlier I quoted Annabel Arden as saying that Schulz and Complicité were 'born for each other', and to this one might take the liberty of adding Lecoq's name as well. Throughout his working life, Lecoq was preoccupied not only with the human body and its movement, but also with matter – its texture, its movement and its relationship to the surrounding space. Both with the neutral mask and through LEM, Lecoq invited his students to explore the properties of life and matter. In the case of neutral mask teaching, this was as a tool of transformation towards dramatic character, while in LEM, however, his attention was focused upon the relationship between objects or bodies and the space they create and disrupt. Lecoq himself might well have spoken The Father's words when he says to Charles: 'I am concerned with this section of space which you are filling' (Théâtre de Complicité 1999: 32). Lecoq brings both the aesthetic concern of a visual artist *and* the pragmatic interest of the theatre-maker to this preoccupation with space, objects and materials – their form, movement and texture. On a number of occasions he talked of his Paris establishment as more of an *art* than a theatre school. We must remember, too, that, until the Nazis banned him from teaching, Schulz had taught art at the local high school in Drohobycz.

At one level, *Crocodiles* seems a celebration of the mysteriously unstable and ever-changing nature of matter. While Schulz's writing invites this, it is clear that Lecoq's legacy provided both McBurney as director and the Complicité actors with a theatre language that gave them the wherewithal to render Schulz's imagery into dramatic form. 'I am fascinated by the movement of things. The whole nature of the way that you integrate the movement of everyday life with action on stage I find obsessively interesting', says McBurney in the *Late Show* documentary. Here, the connection between Lecoq, Schulz and Complicité becomes manifest. These Schulz stories are an obvious, but nonetheless challenging, vehicle in which a company such as Complicité could test Lecoq's ideas and extend some of his teaching principles into the practice of constructing a piece of theatre. I am not suggesting that this was ever a conscious strategy on the part of McBurney and his colleagues when working on *Crocodiles*, but it does not seem too fanciful to propose that, de facto, this is what was happening as they collectively created the work.

Notions of transformation, metamorphosis and mutation are the currency of acting, but Lecoq's interest, as we have seen, extends well beyond the representation of role: the actor's metamorphosis into character. For Lecoq, and for those who choose to embrace his principles, the scope of the actor's job is much wider and extends into the imaginative – rather than purely mimetic – representation of life. Here, actors must have the skill, confidence and imagination to transform themselves into objects, materials and any non-human life form that the texts of the piece require. Complicité's work has long been associated with this quality and in *Crocodiles* the scope for such mutation is considerable. The following represent some examples of script and action from the production:

- As school chairs are raised above the actors' heads a classroom becomes a forest.
- In a scene recalling Joseph's early days as a teacher of carpentry, blocks of wood become alive, taking on a life of their own as these

stage instructions reveal: 'Emil's wood which he has dropped on to the floor, leaps back into his hands. Everyone wants to try this out. Wood and tools and chairs fall everywhere' (Théâtre de Complicité 1999: 15).

• A scene entitled *Father's Beautiful Shop* physically engages the performers in the textural qualities of the cloth to be found in this draper's business. Two staging instructions make the point: 'The cloth begins to move. Emil, Charles, Agatha and Maria move with it, apparently knocked off balance by its beauty. This rapidly leads to a dance.' And: 'He passes his hand over the cloth. It makes a ringing sound' and the Father says: 'If you fold the cloth according to the principles it will emit a sound like a descending scale' (Théâtre de Complicité 1999: 25).

• Books apparently being read by the characters, undulating from their spines, become flapping birds.

• At a dinner table, spoons, forks and plates begin to vibrate and jump, animated playfully by the actors, but as if they had suddenly acquired a life-force of their own.

My argument here is that we can detect overlapping preoccupations between Schulz, Lecoq and Complicité in relation to objects and bodies and their movement in space. Notwithstanding McBurney's protestations about how 'utterly ridiculous' (*Late Show*) it was to make theatre from Schulz's stories, there is something strongly theatrical in Schulz's ideas and their articulation through his fictions. Writer, Jonathan Romney, offers a link to Artaud and the avant-garde:

> The reason Schulz's stories lend themselves so brilliantly to the stage is because they offer . . . [a] manifesto of theatre practice – take his key passages about objects, append them to everything Artaud has to say about human actors, and you have the heart of 20th century avant-garde in a nutshell.
>
> (Romney 1999)

SHARING A POLITICS OF THE IMAGINATION: LECOQ AND COMPLICITÉ

In the inextricable journey from the physical to the creative; in considering how Complicité *prepares* for work; and in the piece's preoccupation with objects and matter, we have identified clear links with Lecoq's thinking and teaching practice. There are other connections, too, which suggest themselves from looking closely at *Crocodiles*. Here, we are investigating an imaginative landscape and theatrical territory where, one supposes, there would have been a strong empathy between Lecoq and Complicité over what the latter was trying to achieve. As analysis of his writing reveals, Lecoq believed unambiguously that a theatre school should have a 'visionary aspect, developing new languages of the stage and thus assisting in the renewal of theatre itself' (Lecoq 2000: 162). More specifically, the 'new theatre of tomorrow' was for him a theatre that did not try to ape the realism of cinema and television. Lecoq was not interested in a theatre which aspired to reproduce – mimetically and literally – the actual conditions of life, rather that, by studying 'life', theatre-makers are in a position to transform it creatively for the stage. A vital clue to this 'visionary aspect' is revealed when he writes about his approach to improvisation:

> We always try to push the situation beyond the limits of reality. We aim for a level of aesthetic reality which would not be recognisable in real life, in order to demonstrate how theatre prolongs life by transposing it. This is a vital discovery for the students.

(Lecoq 2000: 34)

Schulz's writing 'transposes reality' for the page and in turn Complicité has transposed this reality a second time for the stage. I believe Lecoq saw *Crocodiles*, but I have no knowledge of his reaction to the piece. I imagine he would have affirmed what he witnessed. For Lecoq and McBurney, the business of transposing reality for theatrical purposes is a celebration of 'collective imagining' and a process of harnessing some very elemental human desires and needs. The 'collective imagining', which transposed the very particular reality of Schulz's world, produced books transformed into birds, school desks as trees, a character who becomes a fly with two forks as antennae, and cloth – 'pure white calaphony from Malabar' – which dances with mysterious power and beauty. And behind these transformations and the words from Schulz's text are the bodies of the performers. The potential for imaginative transformation of these bodies has been prepared – directly or indirectly – by the creative pedagogy of Lecoq and his teachers. McBurney links this to the latent power of theatre:

> If theatre is to have power it is when it manages to touch on what is a primal
> and universal human need. Words emanate from a physical act in the body,
> and for me the body is where you begin in the rehearsal room.
>
> (McBurney 1999b: 70)

Complicité shares with Lecoq a willingness to invoke a spirit of *universality*. When Lecoq talks of a 'universal poetic sense' (2000: 46) and McBurney of a 'universal human need' and 'unifying people through a common language' (1999b: 75), we sense that they may inhabit the same territory. This is a dramatic landscape constructed upon common principles – or in Lecoq's words 'driving motors' – and which has an ethical preoccupation with the power of theatre to break down barriers, to act as a unifying force. While one senses that neither Lecoq nor McBurney are disposed to employ the language of *universality* with the same fervour as, for example, Peter Brook, they all broadly share the same humanist concerns. Space does not allow further analysis of the issue at this juncture, but I return to it again in the Conclusion.

Regardless of the debate around universalism, what *Crocodiles* embodies in particular, and what Complicité's work seems to represent more generally, is a fusion between the politics of internationalism and the politics of the imagination. Thematically, much of Complicité's recent work seems – at one level – to have explored different elements of the European experience. *Crocodiles*, *The Visit*, *Out of a House Walked a Man*, *The Three Lives of Lucy Cabrol* and – most recently – *Mnemonic*, in varying degrees, have all used the mechanics of memory to explore how the imagination can be harnessed to explore this history. Lecoq is not particularly interested in either the veracity of memory, or in his students using memory to dredge up personal histories. However, where memory plays a crucial part in his teaching is as a trigger for the imagination – a spur towards improvisation and as an impulse for play. It is here that there is evidently common ground between his pedagogy and the strategies Complicité used to create *Crocodiles*. *Crocodiles*, *The Three Lives of Lucy Cabrol* and *Mnemonic* are very different pieces of theatre, but, apart from the same rigorous attention to the physical language(s) of performance, they also share a concern with the particularities of 'ordinary' lives. Perhaps one consistent concern with most of Complicité's work from the early 1980s to the present has been to play with the internal imaginations of apparently mundane lives.

Crocodiles seems particularly to delight in rendering the ordinary, extra-ordinary and the extraordinary, ordinary. Probably, Lecoq never used the phrase 'the politics of the imagination', but that seems as good a way as any of identifying the spirit of much of what he aspired to let loose in the lives of his students.

In an interview for a book of essays investigating the 'spirit of inno-vation' within British theatre in the 1990s, McBurney identified the particular things he learned from Lecoq:

> There are two things really. One is an analysis through the use of movement of how a piece of theatre works: how it actually functions in terms of space, in terms of rhythm, almost like music in terms of counterpoint, harmony: image and action, movement and stillness, words and silence. And having clarified the scaffolding of the building of theatre, he was a wonderful teacher in the stimulation of his pupils' imaginations and the celebration of their individual different imaginations within the context of theatre.

> (McBurney 1994: 18)

Crocodiles seems to have been constructed in a manner which harnesses many of these qualities.

THE CASE OF MUMMENSCHANZ

Mummenschanz – meaning literally 'a play with masks, a play with coincidence' – was established in 1972, becoming publicly visible with its first show at the Avignon Festival. Mummenschanz's founder members were Bernie Schürch, Floriana Frassetto and Andres Bossard. Confronted with the tragedy of Bossard's early death in March 1992, the other two had serious doubts about whether the work should continue. However, after considerable turmoil, Schürch and Frassetto decided to rebuild the company, and in due course recruited John Charles Murphy and Rafaella Mattioli as additional performers.

Bernie Schürch and Andres Bossard met at Lecoq's school in 1967 and until 1972 performed together, initially as clowns and then with a show entitled 'Masks and Buffooneries'. Performing in Rome in 1971, they met Floriana Frassetto, who soon joined them to create Mummen-schanz. Frassetto had trained at an acting academy and with the Roy Besier mime school in Rome between 1968 and 1970. While from 1978

Figure 3.1 Mummenschanz: the slinky

until the early 1990s Mummenschanz consisted of several touring troupes, the permanent creative centre of the company was always Bossard, Frassetto and Schürch.

Mummenschanz is now over thirty years old. Remarkably, during this period the basic dramatic structure and frame of their work – using everyday materials as 'masks' – have remained unchanged. A Mummenschanz show in 2003 is as instantly recognisable – in terms of its form and style – as the work produced in the early 1970s. This is not to suggest that there are no changes, but clearly the company's core members believe that they have yet to exhaust the creative and theatrical potential of the form they first chose to explore in 1972. What exactly this form is and how it works dramatically will be investigated later in this chapter.

In terms of dramaturgical choices, subjects explored and the theatrical languages employed, Théâtre de Complicité and Mummenschanz could hardly be more different. That both companies can trace an inheritance to Lecoq's school graphically illustrates the argument proposed throughout this account, namely that Lecoq never taught a *style* of theatre, rather that he offered a basic lexicon of dramatic possibilities for would-be actors on the one hand, and, on the other, a set of dispositions – or attitudes – that he believed were essential for successful theatre making. Moreover, like the founder members of Complicité, Bossard, Schürch and Frassetto were always ready to acknowledge a debt to Lecoq and talk of his influence. Schürch neatly summarises Lecoq's powers of observation:

> He could somehow scan the students by looking at them, seeing them for a short while and already knowing which way they would react best. Often, his criticisms were just two words and you went home to figure out what you did wrong. . . . He would never show you how things were to be done, and he always addressed 'your work'. He never said 'you' as a person. . . . He never came close. He never praised you: just gave you a push in the right direction. That was his genius as a teacher.
>
> (Schürch and Frassetto 2002)

Bossard and Schürch were in Paris during the tumultuous years of 1968 and 1969: a time when, for a fleeting moment, one could dream – or dread – that an anti-capitalist revolution was on the verge of taking

Figure 3.2 Mummenschanz: hand

place in some leading Western countries. In France there was a general strike and students occupied the Sorbonne and other universities in Paris. As we have seen, this was the period when, as a response to the demands of his own students, Lecoq introduced the *auto-cours*. It was evidently a measure of the affection and respect his students held for him that Lecoq's school continued to function throughout the upheavals. Schürch recalls the atmosphere:

> The spring of '68 had a great impact on the school. We were questioning every-thing. . . . *Why do you teach this? What does it mean? Why do you think we should learn this?* We took advantage of the situation to look for new ways of addressing problems. . . . We were engaged in many activities during that time – also pushed and supported by Lecoq – like going to entertain factory pickets. We supported them morally with entertainment.
>
> (Schürch and Frassetto 2002)

Bossard and Schürch had entered the school already with an interest in mask work, but the experience there allowed them to leave not only with enhanced skills, but with confidence to feel that they must continue to develop this practice: 'What mask has not yet been seen? What mask can we propose?' (Roy and Carasso 1999). Comments like those above hint at that undemonstrative radicalism which Lecoq occasionally allows us to glimpse. In Roy and Carasso's film, Schürch suggests that Lecoq was happy to allow his politics to speak through the work of the school:

> We wanted to abolish the monopolies, the statutes, the institutions. We wanted to take them down from their pedestal, and say, now this is another world. Now it's us! I strongly believe that this was due to Lecoq's influence: to go towards the unreasonable, to go beyond the conceivable.
>
> (Roy and Carasso 1999)

I will consider below some of the more specific influences on Mummenschanz's work which may be identified from Lecoq's teaching. However, the relationship between the two is well encapsulated by Schürch's observation in conversation with me: 'my impression is that Lecoq has greatly influenced not *what* we do, but *how* we go about it. What you do, you find out on your own' (Schürch and Frassatto 2002).

SCULPTORS OF THE IMAGINATION: THE WORK
OF MUMMENSCHANZ

Essentially, Mummenschanz has made three shows in three decades: one new piece of work every ten years. While this is a very misleading statistic, because it does not account for teaching, extensive worldwide touring, collaborative theatre or opera projects and work for television and film, it does reveal the company's refusal to be forced into the normal commercial cycles of theatre production. It also indicates Mummenschanz's demand for a lengthy period of gestation – research and development – for each new major project.

Sometimes – unsatisfactorily – labelled *mime* or *pantomime*, Mummenschanz's work is difficult to define within the normal terminology of performance. Moreover, it fits very uneasily into the fashionable idioms of physical or visual theatre. It is mask work, but unrecognisable from the traditional forms of expressive, *commedia* or Greek chorus masks. What its more recent work certainly provokes is a redrafting of the boundaries between masked performance and puppetry. Prosaically, one might choose to say that all its productions are an investigation – and subsequent animation – of the properties and performative qualities of everyday materials and objects. Such a dry description, however, offers little sense of what is actually happening on stage during a Mummenschanz performance.

The starting point for all their live performance work is the material world – no desire to tell a story, engage with a topical issue or theme, no play script, poem or novel as first impulse, and no apparent interest in displaying that kind of muscular physical theatre for which some contemporary companies are renowned. One writer summarised elements from the company's first production thus: 'it is a curious blend of masks and body-disguising costumes, anthropomorphic creatures, human abstractions and symbolic confrontations' (Cocuzza 1979: 4). For each new project there is a lengthy and unhurried period of preparation, during which materials are gathered from markets, skips, department stores and industrial suppliers, their properties explored and potential for dramatic expression considered. Lycra, foam rubber, styrofoam, plastic tubes and membranes, putty and dough have all regularly been used to create malleable masks, huge balloon-like objects, grotesque body suits and silhouetted body shapes held in front of the performer. Materials and objects are played with endlessly until a theatrical idea begins to take shape. If this pleases the company a proto-type is then constructed, so that the feasibility and logistics of the idea can be tested on stage. At this point it may be found that the object or material is in fact impossible to control with any confidence or clarity, and it is consequently rejected. If, however, it passes this 'test', then the Mummenschanz performers will start to play again with their creation and slowly map out a sequence of moves and emotional states or relationships which they feel have theatrical potential.

Each Mummenschanz show contains a number of scenes or sequences lasting up to seven or eight minutes. These are self-contained and could – apparently – be presented in any order. Although each sequence may contain a simple narrative structure, there is no thematic connec-tion between them. In terms of formal structure, one can begin to identify patterns and dramatic shapes common to a number of the sequences. While every subsequent Mummenschanz show presents un-seen materials and fresh configurations of objects, some have been performed before and now are simply modified and taken further for the latest project. The giant 'slinky' tube, for example, has gone through various stages in its life history and remains one of the company's most powerful creations (Figure 3.1). Similarly, the soft masks made of dough or putty that are reconfigured by the actors in performance first appeared in the early 1970s. The first major show contained many constructions which masked the face, or head and shoulders. The second programme, first performed around 1984, was characterised by larger masks or disguises in which the human frame could hardly be identified at all (Figure 3.2). Sometimes these were enormous baggy balloons propelled around the stage by the performer inside, but unrecognisable as masks in the conventional sense. Some sequences were content to be pure abstractions with no attempt to convey meaning or story line, while others played with emotional content and offered very simple narrative structures. Even here, however, the dramatic structure was deliberately open to interpretation and reading. The company's latest project, which has been performed for over two years, contains recog-nisable elements from previous work, but with new departures – for example, into rubber or foam whole-body masks which are held by the performers in front of their bodies Figures 3.3 and 3.4).

These then are some of the contours of a Mummenschanz perform-ance. In terms of audience relationships and theatrical purpose, what is the company hoping to achieve? At the centre of their practice lies the belief that this wordless play with objects and materials is infinitely communicable, and their continuing popularity around the world gives some credence to such a claim. While Schürch and Frassetto are clearly fascinated by the form and texture of materials, they are not content simply to construct work that communicates itself purely on an aesthetic level. On one hand, they aspire to identify and reveal certain 'universal truths' through their manipulation and animation of the objects and, on the other, they strive to inject an emotional charge into the space created between performers, materials and their audience. Threading through all this is the potential the performers hope they have created for humorous and comic recognition among spectators. In Kamal Musale's film, *The Musicians of Silence*, Schürch comments that the 'secret of Mummenschanz is that we open up the total truth of the moment'. Later he adds: 'we want to entertain people and make them happy. It's the joy of playing' (Musale 2001). These claims and aspirations will be considered in more detail, and in relation to Lecoq's influence, in the sections that follow.

There are at least four areas of Mummenschanz's practice, where either a Lecoq imprint is still visible, or where connections in terms of disposition and stance can be identified. As with the case of Théâtre de Complicité, these links are not reducible to 'cause and effect' relationships, but must be regarded as either a degree of shared orientation, or where a particular Lecoq attitude can be traced within the practice:

1   A consistent preoccupation with creating a theatre vocabulary based upon movement, masks and the manipulation of objects.
2   A commitment to *play* as the motor of creativity.
3   An unapologetic affirmation of popular theatre forms.
4   A willingness to invoke a belief in the possibility of creating universal theatre languages that transcend differences of class, culture and race.

Masks and movement

Bossard and Schürch had already started to explore mask work before joining Lecoq's school in 1967, but as the latter recorded in an interview for the *Mime Journal* in 1974, 'the real flip' happened there. Clearly, whatever else they achieved at the school, the experience of being taught by Lecoq gave both men the confidence and passion to

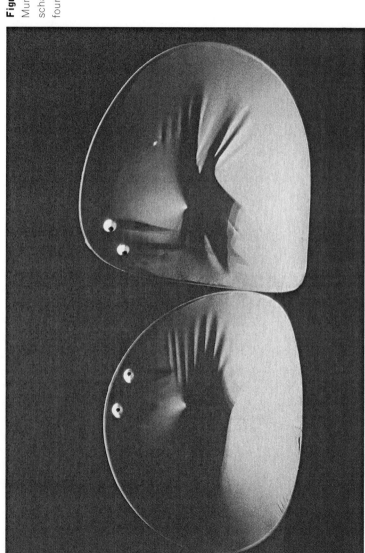

Figure 3.3
Mummen-
schanz:
four eyes

commit themselves to decades of working only with masks. Although they will have learned the principles of different forms of mask work from Lecoq, it is the larval mask that seems to offer the most obvious connections with a style of performance we associate with Mummenschanz. Unlike the neutral mask, the larval mask is a performance tool which – coincidentally – was invented for the carnival of Basel in Switzerland during the mid-1960s. John Wright succinctly identifies the properties and dispositions of the larval mask and considers how Lecoq used it:

> The larval mask discovers the world but does not necessarily make any sense of it. . . . [It] can be mercurial and potentially anarchic in a most endearing way, but the outstanding characteristic of this mask is its insatiable appetite for play. With the larval mask Lecoq confronts his students with the task of finding the corporeal impression from a shape. . . . The larval masks require sensitivity rather than precision, and games rather than accuracy.
>
> (Wright 2002: 79)

Although many of the masks and disguises used by the company over three decades look nothing like the larval masks pictured in *The Moving Body*, many of the properties ascribed to it by John Wright seem perfectly to fit the behaviour of the objects and materials in a typical Mummenschanz show. Mummenschanz has taken the spirit of Lecoq's original larval mask and invested it in the eclectic range of materials and constructions created since 1972. The questions Lecoq asked of these larval masks in the Paris school concerning movement, space, rhythm, speed and direction are of the same order as those posed by Bossard, Frassetto and Schürch to the tubes, beanbag balloons, cardboard boxes, foam rubber full-body masks, putty masks and toilet rolls, which have formed just part of the Mummenschanz repertoire over thirty years. Clearly, too, the company's process of research and devising has always paid heed to Lecoq's dictum that 'masked performance requires an indispensable distance between the mask and the actor's face. For that reason the mask must be larger (or smaller) than the actor's face' (Lecoq 2000: 55).

The starting – and often finishing – point for a sequence with, say, a very large bag with a mischievous propensity to float is a controlled exploration of its movement properties. These scenes seem to be at their most effective when the performers inject as little narrative as possible on the apparently abstract movement dynamics of the material in question. Where the performers impose a self-conscious personality – or romantic narrative – on the business, there is a danger that the spectator's interpretative options are closed down, and the anthropomorphism becomes unduly sentimental.

The movement and rhythmic dynamic imposed by each of these various masks makes considerable physical demands on the performers, involving their whole bodies. Members of the company organise their own physical preparation – there is no attempt to impose a Mummenschanz movement 'technique' class, although in the early 1980s, at the behest of Frassetto, a dance choreographer was brought in to tackle what the performers admitted was a 'nonchalant' approach towards physical preparation. Today, although in their fifties, the performers keep in good shape, but largely follow their own routines of movement preparation. Bossard echoes Lecoq's insistence that movement preparation remain linked to creative work in a comment: 'when I exercise, I find plenty of inspiration. Movement is a source of ideas. I learned that from Lecoq' (Bührer 1984: 65).

Arguably, the Mummenschanz project for thirty years has been an undeviating exploration and application of the principles of Lecoq's larval masks – disguises that offer almost unlimited possibilities for fantasy and imaginative reveries. Lecoq writes about two dimensions of research into larval masks. Following work on characters and situations, the dimensions of animality and fantasy are investigated: 'this research leads to the discovery of a strange, undefined and unknown population. This exploration of the incomplete body, inevitably different, opens up the imaginary realm' (Lecoq 2000: 59.) Just such 'a strange, undefined and unknown population' seems to have colonised every Mummenschanz show.

Play

Like Théâtre de Complicité and numerous performers who trained with either Lecoq or Gaulier, Mummenschanz invokes the crucial importance of *play*. For Frassetto and Schürch, play or playfulness not only drives their creative journey in the devising and rehearsal process, but also defines the actors' relationship to their masks in performance. It signals, too, the kind of relationship the company hopes to achieve with its audience:

The playfulness of human beings seems to be inherent. We always like to be playful – it is the common denominator around the world. We often say that the stage is our playground. We play with these shapes and objects, and the audience is invited to *join* us on stage and play with these figures too, adding their own stories and associations.

(Schürch and Frassetto 2002)

While Schürch is usually speaking metaphorically about the audience joining them on stage, that spirit of collusion between artists and spectators is clearly very important to the company. Despite the strangeness of the objects, the often abstract nature of dramatic material, and that this work is far removed from the conventions of naturalism and realism, Mummenschanz is seeking a sense of empathy and identification from its audiences. This – they hope – will happen partly through humorous recognition, and partly through a loose emotional correspondence between spectator and the circumstances in which the masks find themselves. Clearly, for Frassetto and Schürch, if their work is to attain a universal level of communication, then it must possess the quality of play and playfulness. Play therefore is a necessary – almost a sufficient – condition for the achievement of such a state. One senses that, for Mummenschanz, play assumes a greater importance than for many companies influenced by the teaching of Lecoq. Given, at one level, the simplicity of its work – no complex narratives, no subtle psychological characterisation and no intricate sound or lighting technology – one might wish to summarise its form as: play + masks = Mummenschanz. While this understates the level of skill and research that is invested in each project, such a formula perhaps encapsulates the essential qualities of how they work, and what we see during a Mummenschanz performance.

Popular theatre

Although Lecoq never explicitly made it his political mission to advocate 'popular theatre', any close reading of what he said suggests sympathy in this direction. He was impatient with what he called 'intellectual theatre', and it is hard to know how he might have reacted to what might be described as postmodern deconstruction in contemporary performance practice. As I have argued above, such a stance should not be read as anti-intellectualism, but more a manifestation of his lifelong commitment to rediscovering, and placing in a contemporary context, the essential corporeal motors of theatrical expression and exchange.

In some ways Mummenschanz's work provides a curious paradigm for 'popular theatre'. It would be possible – and not entirely inappropriate – to locate the company's practice historically in the high modernist tradition of the visual arts avant-garde. One could look at a Mummenschanz performance and identify the play of abstract shapes and sounds with the forms one associates with Futurism, Dada, Surrealism and the Bauhaus. Perhaps, too, in its yearning for a simpler, more emotionally truthful and less complicated world, the fantastical imagery conjured up by the Mummenschanz performers speaks of aspirations similar to those articulated by the *enfants terribles* of early twentieth-century avant-garde movements. However, if Mummenschanz has a mission to subvert, it is as a result of liberating the imagination of its audiences through play and the pleasures to be derived from visual stimulation. Tom Leabhart neatly maps the transition of imagery from modernist avant-garde to popular visual theatre on Broadway or in Zurich during the final decades of the twentieth century: 'it is as if, suddenly, fifty years of rather difficult material, research that had a dangerous edge, had been rendered respectable, amusing and even appropriate for children. . . . Most audiences recognise and respond to the anecdotal dynamism beneath the abstracted forms' (Leabhart 1989: 105). Whatever politically agitational ideas the founder members of the company harboured in the late 1960s and early 1970s, today their ambitions are simpler. Schürch and Frassetto summarise what their current hopes are in terms of audience response:

> You start off by wanting to change the world, but then slowly you come down to saying if we can give the audience something that they can feel – whether it is happiness or sadness – that's good enough.
>
> Laughter is the reason to go on. To hear children laughing. I am not going to change anyone's life and point my finger and say 'think this or that'. Just trying to awaken the pureness of those emotions is enough.
>
> (Schürch and Frassetto 2002)

Although children figure significantly within their audiences, the Mummenschanz performers believe that their work communicates itself effectively to any adult who is open enough to embrace its playful spirit. A Mummenschanz show is not 'popular theatre' in the particular sense of being both popular and possessing a sharp political perspective. However, the longevity of the company, and its ability still to play to capacity audiences in middle- or large-scale theatres in Europe and North America attest to another kind of popularity – a popularity which acknowledges the entertainment value of the work and its ability to spark and liberate the imagination.

Universal communication

The observations quoted in the box below represent a range of claims made by the Mummenschanz founders, or – as in the case of the comment by Bari Rolfe – a quality ascribed to them. If one attempts to distil these various statements, it seems that the company's ability to reach a universal level of communication through its work rests on a number of propositions (listed below).

- Human movement has the potential to communicate itself universally.
- It is possible to find – or create – a fundamental language of theatre that can be understood anywhere.
- Certain emotions and gestures have the power to be understood universally.
- An instinct – or a disposition – for play is a phenomenon that exists across different cultures.

Some or all of these claims have been common currency for a significant number of artists or theatre-makers throughout the twentieth century. While such issues have particularly been on the agenda for disciplines such as anthropology, sociology and cultural studies, they have – by and large – been ignored within theatre studies and drama until relatively recently. It is beyond the scope of this account to investigate the validity of these ideas in any depth, although the book's Conclusion takes the matter slightly further in relation to Lecoq himself. As summarised above, they seem to embody a more extensive and unambiguous series of beliefs than those articulated by Lecoq in his writing. The extent to which Lecoq might put his name – without qualification – to these ideas is debatable. Here, the point is to signal these claims, both as questions for reflection and further discussion, and as markers that situate Mummenschanz's work in relation to that of other companies in time and place.

LECOQ AND MUMMENSCHANZ: AFTERTHOUGHTS

The relationship between Mummenschanz and Lecoq continued to be a significant one until his death. He is invoked regularly throughout Bührer's book on the company, and at one point is quoted at length. Characteristically, he mixes praise for the originality of their work with an honest and sharp observation about the dangers of their considerable success at the end of their first major project:

> With them, there are no set characters; it's something else, a silent poetry, with humour besides . . . a very personal sense of humour. When those two grey putty heads join and become one, it says so much, the impossibility to break off after coming together. It's extraordinary poetically speaking. . . . Their success is quite unique. To succeed on Broadway can be dangerous. They

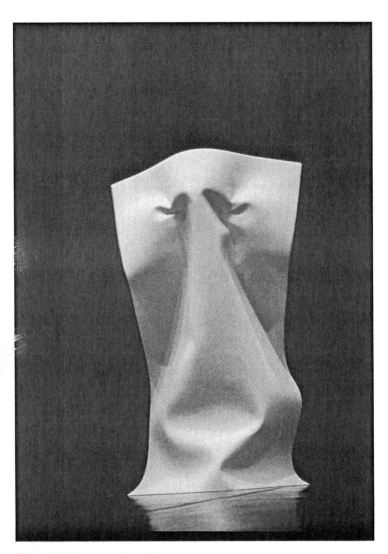

Figure 3.4 Mummenschanz: the nose

were almost too successful; they didn't know what to do about it. I often advised
the Mummenschanz: do another show, a different one; don't be scared, even
if it's not as good as the first one. . . . It's very hard to stop and question oneself
when things are working well.

(Bührer 1984: 40)

Quoted at some length, this comment illustrates Lecoq's continuing
concern for his ex-pupils, affirming some particularly effective dimensions of the work, but then jolting them with a warning about
complacency. There is no record of how Lecoq responded to Mummenschanz's second major project, and whether indeed he thought it
was 'different' and 'as good as the first one'. Regardless of his actual
feelings, that he chose to identify Mummenschanz with only a few
other companies in 'New perspectives', the final chapter of *The Moving
Body* evidences his high regard for the innovative quality of its work.
He writes that 'looking back, I recall especially the work of the
Mummenschanz whose research into masks and forms has been far-
reaching' (Lecoq 2000: 161).

4

PRACTICAL
EXERCISES

In this part of the book – as with all the others in the series – I present
a sequence of practical exercises designed to offer both student and
teacher a distilled, but nonetheless physical and somatic, experience of
Lecoq's teaching. In certain crucial ways this was the most challenging
and difficult chapter to write, for it posed a number of awkward questions. For example:

*   How can I attempt to capture the richness and complexity of
    Lecoq's pedagogy – honed over fifty years – in one short
    chapter?
*   Given that Lecoq did not offer either a *system* or a *method* and that
    – as he constantly stressed – his teaching proposed a *journey* of
    discovery for each student, how can this spirit – and sense of trav-
    elling – be captured through the written pages of a book?
*   How can a teaching process, the success of which is premised on
    the teacher having both a deep knowledge of the body, how it
    moves and an extraordinary sensitivity to each individual student's
    strengths and weaknesses not only as actor, but as playful 'liver of
    life', be captured and conveyed by someone with lesser experi-
    ence?
*   Mindful of Simon McBurney's comments in his foreword to *The
    Moving Body*, how can I avoid reducing this section to a banal and

mechanistic 'instruction manual' (Lecoq 2000: x), no different in essence to one which tells you how to programme your video recorder or change an electric plug?

The short and truthful answer to the first three questions is that a series of practical exercises articulated in written form within a chapter of a book can never substitute for the lived experience of a face-to-face encounter with the originator of such a pedagogy. The danger in reproducing all the sensual excitement of an instruction manual is self-evidently a risk, and McBurney's warning remains a stark reminder of the hazards of such an endeavour. Nonetheless, if transparent limitations are placed upon the ambition of the task and no claims are offered that it represents a proper substitute for attending Lecoq's school in Paris, then the undertaking remains, I believe, a worthwhile and achievable one. Moreover, what this project can do is to give both teachers and students of theatre a sense – a flavour – of the journey on which Lecoq and his fellow teachers led thousands of students over a forty-five-year period. The sequences that follow may, for many of you, represent an approach to actor training that is startlingly different from the normal routines offered at drama school, college or university. If pursued with thoroughness and due attention to the detail of the written instructions, the experience will – if nothing else – provide a preparation and sensitising of the body for theatre. Beyond this, leading yourself – or being guided – through these exercises should provide a clear sense of the physical *connectedness* between basic human actions – pushing and pulling, for example – and the dramatic territories of tragedy, melodrama and *commedia dell'arte*.

What follows was conceived and constructed with Thomas Prattki who, at the time of writing, was teaching at the Lecoq school. Prattki started working with Lecoq in 1993 and from October 1999 – Lecoq died in January of the same year – became Director of Pedagogy. Prattki has now left the Paris school and will be setting up his own establishment in London in 2003. Over a number of visits to Paris during 2001 and 2002, I had conversations with Prattki, not only concerning the challenge of this 'practical exercises' chapter, but also about many other aspects of Lecoq's philosophy and teaching. After debating various options, Prattki proposed that this section chapter present a *microcosm* of the educational journey offered by Lecoq and his colleagues at the school. Here, rather than identify a set of written instructions on how to run a 'Lecoq workshop' on, for example, the neutral mask, the clown or *bouffons*, he suggested that, from the fundamental human movements of pushing and pulling, we trace three short practical journeys – through exercises and improvisation – into the dramatic territories of melodrama, tragedy and *commedia dell'arte*. While each of these journeys offers a distilled, though genuine sense of how Lecoq worked at the school, they are not exact reproductions of classes taught by him. Prattki has offered his own slant on these exercises and – of course – it is important to stress that, standing alone, these three sections do not offer a complete guide for the theatre student of how to create melodrama, tragedy or the *commedia dell'arte*. However, what these exercises provide, in their somatic interrogation of different permutations of pulling and pushing, is a strong sense of the movement dynamics – *the motors* – which lie embedded within three of the dramatic territories that Lecoq taught during the second year of the school's curriculum.

AIMS

- To provide a distillation of some of the key principles of Lecoq's approach to teaching theatre and acting.
- To experience somatically two specific, but fundamental, Lecoq principles: (a) movement provokes emotion, and (b) the body remembers.
- To experience and understand an educational journey from basic movements through emotional states into three *territories* of theatre or drama.
- To experience the driving forces – the movement dynamics – of tragedy, melodrama and *commedia dell'arte*.

BACKGROUND AND CONTEXT

Two fundamental principles are inherent in these exercises:

- Movement provokes emotion
- The body remembers

The school believes in a strong link between movement and emotion, and avoids any separation between *movement* technique and *acting* classes. It is always the intention at the school to establish links between activities that are often regarded as unconnected. Thus a first-year class in physical preparation points forward to second-year work on the main dramatic territories. Here, an approach to movement aims to extend students' physical awareness, while simultaneously creating a resource for future work on emotional states. Consequently, the school does not offer separate classes in dance, voice or acrobatics, for example, but is more interested in the driving forces behind each theatrical style. The dramatic territories of tragedy, melodrama or *commedia* each offer a separate space in which to uncover different dynamic motors. Who pushes, who pushes himself, or is pushed? At the school the students' work will be a precise analysis of these driving forces that – at a later date – will help them to avoid clichés and provide a deeper under- standing of the dynamics of each territory. Thus, armed with knowledge that blends a corporeal and cognitive understanding of these embedded dynamics, students will be in a position to reinvent these dramatic territories for the 'theatre of tomorrow'. It is salutary to remind ourselves once again that Lecoq was not demanding that his students simply reproduce these traditions for the modern stage, but that they should *remember* the conventions of each so as to be able to change and reformulate them for the contemporary world.

APPROACH

Primarily, as the title of the chapter implies, these exercises are for *doing* – for trying out – in practice. They may simply be read, however, along with the rest of the book, as a means of further deepening the reader's understanding of Lecoq's teaching and theoretical principles. Nonetheless, everything that follows is written assuming that these tasks are for physical practice in a studio, rather than for the calming delight of reflection and intellectual contemplation. Our expectation is that, normally, a tutor experienced in the teaching of drama, theatre studies or the performing arts will lead these three sequences. However, it is quite possible for a self-directed group of students to work through these sequences themselves. In such a case, it is important that one or two participants are designated 'tutor' to fulfil the function of 'outside eye' and to ensure that the instructions are followed accu- rately. Each main sequence pursues the same basic structure: physical preparation, improvisation and a third unit entitled 'into the dramatic territories . . .'. The third unit may contain both improvisations and exercises. They need to be conducted in a structured context and will not be effective if only the most apparently pleasing or seductive elements of the programme are selected.

In order that the experience is maximised for all participants, the following points are offered as guidelines for the planning and teaching of these exercises:

- *Preparing space and students*: You should wear clothes that allow for easy movement. The chosen space should be as free of material *clutter*, extraneous noise and distraction as possible.

- *Planning the sessions*: These exercises are presented in three separate sections. While each section is an entity in its own right, each task and the sections themselves should be taught in the order presented. Provided the exercises are taught in the sequence which follows, they may be spread out over a number of days or weeks. No recommendations are given for the duration of each exercise, as this will depend on various factors, and particularly upon the size of the student group.

- *Taking time*: While there are always limitations on available time, tutors are encouraged not to rush these exercises. Sometimes the body learns slowly and often the most interesting discoveries occur only after you have been working on a specific task for a while – much longer perhaps than may have at first seemed necessary. The threshold of boredom can be the point at which genuine learning and real discovery takes place.

- *Precision and accuracy*: While an imaginative and confident tutor will always be open to unscheduled, but relevant, creative diversions, it is important that attention is given to the accuracy and detail of each instruction, and how it is executed by the student. Each exercise and its component parts are born out of years of practice and revision at Lecoq's school. If they are conducted in a general manner that only approximates to the instruction, the corresponding benefit and learning will be dissipated and weakened.

- *Talk and discussion*: Try to keep any discussion and comment on the process separate from the time allocated for the practical work.

While discussion and debate have their place, the impact and effect of these exercises cannot be measured or evaluated through 'intellectual' analysis. As must be evident by now, much of Lecoq's work is registered – initially at least – corporeally. As the body moves and learns new physical actions or sequences other elements of human capability and understanding are brought into play.

- *Neutral mask*: As we have discovered in an earlier part of this book, the neutral mask is a pedagogical tool of considerable power, and some of the initial exercises in each of these three sections presuppose its use. A short section below indicates some preliminary exercises that can be undertaken with students to introduce them to the principles of the neutral mask. However, Prattki and I were well aware that many theatre teachers would not have access to neutral masks. Consequently, these exercises *can* be undertaken without employing the neutral mask; although, where available, they should be used as indicated. Where exercises would benefit from the neutral mask, the phrase is appended in parentheses at the end of each instruction.

The incremental development of the activities has been carefully considered, and therefore it is essential that they be taught in the order presented below.

PREPARATORY EXERCISES

A: PREPARING FOR THE NEUTRAL MASK

The neutral mask is only a teaching and learning tool; it is very rarely worn in performance. Unlike a character mask, which has its inner conflicts, the neutral mask aims to achieve a state of calm without tension or contradiction. Since this mask aspires to being open, available and ready to respond to the world it encounters, the actor must be prepared to engage willingly with that world – a world that moves and will move him. Each encounter with the world creates a state of off-balance, since we experience something new and unknown. Human beings seem to possess a strong inner dynamic that creates a tension between a desire to enjoy the provocation of instability, and a fear of what this state of off-balance may bring. The neutral mask allows the actor to recognise – in a playful way – that the experience of calmness and openness can be achieved only by accepting the perpetual motion between balance and off-balance. The neutral mask invites the actor to enjoy the pleasure of going off-balance so as to find a new balance, to go off-balance again to discover a new balance, and so on. . . . An actor who needs to play the inner conflicts of a character must at first experience a state of calm openness in order to be capable of later playing the dramatic 'off-balance'.

Exercise: Moving off-balance

These simple exercises, presented in four linked parts, are *preparation* for working with the neutral mask. They are *not* conducted wearing the neutral mask. You should all experience this off-balance exercise, whether or not you will work with neutral masks later in the sequence. The exercise is useful in conveying a *sense* of what can be achieved through working with the neutral mask.

Exercise 4.1

➤ *Part I*: Working in groups of three with one person between two others – one in front, one behind, and keeping both feet firmly placed on the ground (including the heels), the person in the centre moves off-balance towards the other one in front. He catches him, pushing him gently back to upright and over in the opposite direction towards the person behind. The actions are repeated. The distance between the off-balance person and the catchers should not be too great. It's not about a deep fall, but experiencing the precise moment when the body goes off-balance.

➤ *Part II*: The exercise above is repeated, but this time the person in the centre *exhales* while going off-balance. The normal reaction would be to inhale because of the fear of falling, a fear of the unknown and of losing control. Encouraging the person moving off-balance to exhale removes tension in the body when encountering the unknown.

➤ *Part III*: Now each of you plays alone with the pleasure of being off-balance. Starting always in a centred and upright position, you should enjoy trying off-balances forwards, sideways and backwards, but catching yourself before falling to the floor. This exercise encourages you to be playful in exploring off-balances.

➤ *Part IV*: Each of you pursues Part III a stage further by taking one step at the very moment you would fall to the floor through being off-balance. By experiencing the simple act of taking one step the body lives the dynamic rhythm of moving off-balance to find a new balance, only to fall off-balance again. . . . While doing the exercise you should avoid looking at the floor, but concentrate on the space that surrounds you. By focusing on the space you may feel that the move to off-balance is a reaction to that space. Unable to remain a mere observer of that space – of life – you wish to be moved by it, through stepping into it. This desire to move on – this state of readiness – should be visible in all parts of your body. If it is, then you are ready to carry the neutral mask.

B: DYNAMICS OF PUSHING AND PULLING

The dynamics of pushing and pulling can be broken down into three pairings, or six distinct units:

- *I push . . . I pull*
- *I am pushed . . . I am pulled*
- *I push myself . . . I pull myself*

This simple exercise introduces you to push–pull dynamics and will provide a platform upon which to analyse the different categories that follow.

Exercise 4.2

➤ Each of you walks in turn across the studio, attempting to repro-duce your normal daily rhythm of movement: no acting, no anecdotes. You may be asked to repeat this several times.

➤ *Observers*: Closely observe the movement of the walking students and reflect on questions such as these:

- Do they push the space, or are they pushed by it?
- Do they have to push themselves through the space, or are they pulled by something?
- Do they push the space with their upper body, while some force pulls the pelvis back?
- What images are generated by the different ways of walking? (Someone who pushes the space may appear powerful; someone who is pushed, reluctant; someone who is pulled, naive. . . .)
- Do diverse ways of walking suggest different emotional states?
- Is it possible to correlate different permutations of pushing and pulling with different emotions?

Tutor notes

From this exercise students should have a sense of (a) their own habitual walking patterns, and (b) an awareness of using push and pull actions to help find a character in different theatrical styles. All *commedia* characters are based on these physical principles. While *commedia* characters – Harlequin, Pantelone, the Captain, for example – demand a very physical approach, this method is also useful in more psychological forms of drama.

When students work with text it is important to register the relationship between words and actions, or physical behaviour. Is the body expressing the same emotion as the words, or do they counterpoint each other? In *commedia* there is sometimes a complete congruence between a character's body and verbal language. However, in many of the other dramatic territories there is often a strong contradiction between body and language. A character might push with words, but the body is pulled back. A character may state that he is not scared, while his body expresses the opposite.

The experience of these two preparatory exercises should act as basic groundwork for tackling the three main areas that follow.

I PUSH . . . I PULL: TOWARDS THE DYNAMICS OF MELODRAMA

PHYSICAL PREPARATION

Exercise 4.3

➤ Work in pairs, one standing in front of the other. The person behind firmly grasps the hips – the pelvis – of the one in front. The person in front leans forward with his entire body, keeping heels on the ground. The person behind must prevent the one being held from falling on the floor, so he pulls the hips backwards. Thus, by pulling in opposite directions you try to find a dynamic balance between yourselves.

➤ *First development* . . . : Sustaining the same dynamic balance, the person in front now tries to walk forward while his partner endeavours to pull him back. Both must use their entire strength either to push forward from the pelvis (into walking), or to pull the other back. What was a dynamic balance between you turns into a dramatic *off balance* since one person will almost certainly be stronger than the other. Thus either the person who is trying to walk cannot do so and is pulled backwards by the stronger partner, or the one behind is pulled forward by the one in front – despite his intentions.

➤ *Second development* . . . : When the partner behind gets tired, he lets go so the one in front is free to walk off. The link between the two is broken. The person in front should continue walking for a while to register the feeling invoked after having struggled to break free from the one behind.

Exercise 4.4

➤ Continue to work in pairs, but now you are given a wooden stick about 120 centimetres long. Bamboo canes would be suitable for this exercise. Facing each other, the stick is supported between the palms of your right hands, so the distance between you will remain constant at about 120 cm. Note that the stick must not be grasped in the hands: it is part of the challenge of this exercise to find the right tension between the two supporting hands, so that the stick will fall if the pressure is relaxed.

➤ Begin to play by pushing each other through the space, but avoid making the game too aggressive, and allow the stick to engage your entire body. Thus, a sensation is generated of being connected in space, but without actually touching each other. Initially, the exercise concerns the pleasure of discovering a wide range of pushing movements between you and your partner, but then begins to take on a more obvious dramatic quality. Here, different emotional states will be generated as one of you, for example, is pushed to the floor or against a wall. What at first was only a playful encounter may easily turn into a violent or passionate relationship. By the end of this exercise, the link between purely physical pulling and pushing, and pulls and pushes that begin to generate emotional states, will have been established.

IMPROVISATION

The Valley of the Giants (neutral mask)

Imagine that you are giants. You must find imaginative ways to share with the audience a vision of how you live as a giant. You are encouraged to engage with objects and materials that are, of course, giant-size too. The improvisation can be explored singly, in pairs or in large groups.

Tutor notes

The physical preparation for pulling and pushing develops here into an improvisation that stimulates a strong physical presence. Pushing and pulling with the entire body should make students feel like giants. Initially in the exercise they will probably come up with typical 'giant clichés', such as walking around the space with heavy steps, or – like *King Kong* – destroying aeroplanes with their bare hands. They should be encouraged to go beyond these clichés and enjoy the fundamental pleasure of large movements and simply of being *big*. The students should be encouraged to engage in activities that allow them to be physically fully present. Since everything is big in The Valley of the Giants, they must engage their *entire bodies* in being big too. This is a useful improvisation that encourages students to have the confidence of enjoying all parts of their bodies in the play of being a giant.

INTO THE DRAMATIC TERRITORIES: MELODRAMA

The physical preparation exercises and improvisation explored above would normally be taught in the first year of Lecoq's programme. In the second year, students will begin to translate these experiences and skills into an exploration of the main dramatic territories of theatre. In this context, students will be able to deepen their understanding of opposing forces that make space dynamic and generate dramatic situations.

Exercise 4.5: charging the space

➤ Working in pairs, face each other about one metre apart. Imagine that you are connected to each other by an invisible string which could be attached to your chests, foreheads or bellies. The string should always be taut, so the distance between you remains constant at one metre. Possibly, an image of a stick is more appropriate than string. At this stage you should not travel around the space.

➤ Thus, if the string or stick is attached to your foreheads, one will move the other by pushing his head forward. In order to keep the string tight – or the stick suspended – the other must respond by pulling back his head. Initially, work slowly with the pushes and pulls so that you really sense the invisible string or stick between you, and so that the distance of a metre between partners is always maintained. As you begin to move forward and back the space between you becomes dramatically dynamic and alive. Once you are confident with this movement, and have established the sensation of the dramatic space, become faster and more ambitious in your pushing and pulling movements.

➤ *First development* . . . : Remain facing each other, but now increase the distance between you to two metres. The idea of pushing and pulling while maintaining a constant distance between you is repeated, but this time begin to travel around the space. Now, too, moments of stillness can be inserted and the 'rules' of the movement relationship can become more fluid.

➤ As you face each other over the two-metre space, one starts to walk towards or away from his partner and stops, immobile. The partner then responds – walking towards or away – and then also stops. A moment of stillness. These points of immobility allow you – and the spectators – to discover that the space remains alive and dynamic even when you are motionless. Gradually, start to vary your rhythm, moving slowly away at one moment, rapidly the next. Perhaps, one moves fast while the other reacts in counterpoint very slowly; one remains still while the other moves away until the link is cut completely. In this part of the exercise all the options are explored while the basic principles are sustained.

➤ *Second development* . . . : The final part of this exercise is to charge the space even more by adding words to your encounter. Initially, whoever moves – pushes – first utters one word before or after the movement, while the other reacts in silence: for example, *Why? Please! Come!* Later, the reacting partner – whoever pulls back – can respond with a word as well. It is important at this stage to avoid entering into a lengthy dialogue. This overcomplicates the exercise and potentially diffuses the charge created in the space.

IMPROVISATION

The Departure

A member of the family (usually son or daughter) leaves home. Different possible reasons might be given to justify the situation: the only son is being called up to go to war; the pregnant daughter has decided to follow her lover who is not accepted by the family; the gay son who has just 'come out' to his family is leaving to live with his boyfriend, etc.

The situation to be improvised is the moment of departure at home just before the person leaves. The family is in the sitting room when the son or daughter enters to say goodbye. The improvisation should be played *in silence*, so as to confront the characters with a situation where no one present needs to say anything. Thus the focus is given to the silent dramatic tension between the characters.

Tutor notes

This improvisation is the culmination of all the earlier exercises and it should be made clear to the students that they are expected to draw upon the knowledge generated through the previous activities. The way the characters push or pull the space reveals different family relationships. Each relationship could be precisely analysed through the way the characters exchange looks, their reactions, and how they move towards, or away from, each other. The drama of the situation will also be revealed by sudden or subtle changes in rhythm.

The characters will discover by themselves their emotional relationship to the departing family member as the improvisation unfolds. Each character should also be aware of all the others, and must be able to respond to any proposal that is forthcoming. Thus, the movement dynamic – the pushing and pulling of space – is not simply between family members and the departing son or daughter, but between all of them.

The most important aspect of this improvisation is that the students learn to construct a dramatic situation, not primarily by focusing on isolated emotional states, but through the dramatic space between the characters created by their emotions. Here, the student is learning how to translate an emotion into dramatic movement within a dramatic situation. The movement might be very small: an invisible smile, a sideways look, a sharp or long inhalation or exhalation of breath. Whatever each performer does or says, he either pushes or pulls the space around him. After each group has completed the improvisation, the tutor may wish to describe and analyse what happened. Who pushed? Who pulled? How did the space become emotionally charged?

I AM PUSHED . . . I AM PULLED: TOWARDS THE DYNAMICS OF TRAGEDY

PHYSICAL PREPARATION

Exercise 4.6

➤ Working in pairs, stand immediately behind your partner. The person in front is the puppet, the one behind, the puppeteer.

The puppeteer provokes movement in the puppet by touching different parts of his body – back or side of the head, shoulders, pelvis, knees, heels, etc. When the puppet's head is pushed slowly forward, for example, the impulse is accepted until the pushing stops. The head then returns to the initial position of departure. As you both become more confident with the game, the puppeteer provokes faster and faster movement, and even different body parts at the same time. The puppet must accept the rhythm offered, always trying to return the moved body part back to the point of departure.

Exercise 4.7

➤ Form a circle of seven people. An additional person is placed in the centre of the circle and then moves slowly to the edge. On reaching the edge, he is pushed back into the centre, only to move out again to the periphery. Initially, the pushes are slow until the person in the centre becomes confident, but as the game progresses the provocations can become more – playfully – violent. The person in the centre should always remain in control of his own body and avoids falling.

Exercise 4.8

➤ You will work on identifying with different materials. The aim is initially to find the physical quality of the material and then to transpose this into a dramatic or emotional quality. The materials selected should undergo a change or development in their state. Thus, for example, a sugar lump melting in a glass of water; a sheet of paper ripped into shreds; a piece of iron attacked by an acid; a raw egg smashed against the wall; or a piece of elastic stretched and released.

➤ Taking the sugar lump as an example, observe the process of sugar dissolving slowly in the water. By the end of the observation, imagine that you *become* the sugar lump as it dissolves into the water. At first, you should only try to embody the observed rhythms of the melting sugar – capturing the rhythmic quality of the process is more important than trying to imitate it. At this point in the exercise do not allow anecdotes, emotional qualities or any 'acting' to creep in.

➤ In the second step, you discover the dramatic qualities of the observed phenomena. Imagine, for example, a person who melts away like a piece of dissolving sugar, and try to capture the physical qualities of this transition. What kind of dramatic quality is provoked when a human body is dissolving like a piece of sugar, exposed to stronger *external* forces?

➤ These steps can be followed using the imagery of other materials suggested above. It is especially important that plenty of time is allotted to the first step, so that you can really begin to inhabit the physical qualities of the materials selected. Spending too little time on this part of the exercise encourages you to contrive – artificially – the dramatic and emotional qualities residing in the material, rather than to embody them in a deep way.

IMPROVISATION

The Journey Through the Elements

This can be conducted individually or in groups. You are invited to imagine yourself on a journey through different and often extreme elements. Tutors may construct their own journey, but the narrative might look like this:

At first you are in the ocean and thrown on to the beach by a huge wave. You cross the beach and enter a forest. While searching for a way out you discover that the forest is on fire and so have to run as fast as possible. Suddenly, you are confronted by a mountain which you must climb to escape the forest fire. As you climb, an earthquake shakes the mountain, but you manage to reach the summit. Stumbling through falling rocks, you descend to emerge safely into a valley. Here you must cross a river, now swollen by a wild torrent. Jumping from stone to stone you cross the river, but on several occasions are swept into the raging waters by the power of the flood. By grabbing on to fallen trees you avoid being swept away, eventually to reach the other side. Now you must cross a desert to reach the city of your destination, but a sandstorm blows up making it impossible to see. Finally, the storm calms and at last you view the city, only to discover it has been ransacked and burned to the ground.

The First Class

This improvisation can be conducted with a large group of students. The theme to be played out follows a new teacher in front of his first class:

> The director of a school presents the new history teacher to his class. After a short introduction the director departs, leaving the teacher alone with his new students. Initially rather shy, the teacher begins on his favourite subject – Napoleon, for example – but soon feels that the class is going rather well. He gains confidence, and the more he continues to share his enthusiasm for the subject with the students, the more passionate he becomes. There comes a point when the passion takes over and, instead of talking about his subject, he begins to live it. The students are forgotten and he is completely captured by the world of his passion. He no longer talks about Napoleon, but he *becomes* Napoleon, reliving the battles, the victories and the love life of the man he admires. In the middle of his biggest victory he is stunned by a paper ball a student throws at his eye. Immediately he falls back into reality, realising that his students are completely bored.

Tutor notes

All this work confronts students with the sensation of being exposed to forces which are much stronger than they are. The physical preparation exercises awaken the sensation of being pushed and pulled, so that the *Journey Through the Elements* improvisation allows students to discover a dramatic situation in an off-balance environment. Here, being pushed and pulled by wild elements constantly exposes students to the physical experience of being thrown off-balance.

The First Class improvisation takes this experience on to a more psychological level. Here, in place of external forces, students are pulled and pushed by forces from within: their own passions. The physical work on identification with different materials goes a step further and opens up a dramatic and tragic space. Being exposed to forces they cannot control, students discover – through theatrical transposition – the sensation of being destroyed in an irreversible way. The dissolved sugar lump, the iron attacked by acid or the egg thrown against a wall will never be the same again. The bodily discovery – sensation – of being pushed and pulled into irreversible destruction opens the door to a physical understanding of dramatic tragedy: the experience of being propelled – pushed and pulled – by the forces of one's own destiny.

INTO THE DRAMATIC TERRITORIES: TRAGEDY

Lecoq's work on tragedy focused on the experience of the chorus and a very physical approach to text. The school continues to work on tragedy in this manner. The sensations generated by being pushed and pulled offer a possible link to tragedy, and the same approach is applied to work on tragic texts.

The following exercises require a choice of appropriate texts to be provided by the tutor and learned in advance by the students. Perhaps three of four short extracts divided among the student group would be appropriate. The choice of texts is important for these exercises: they should be chosen so as to offer rich material in terms of physical provocation and evocation. Certain Shakespearean or Greek texts may be suitable, as would more modern scripts from writers such as Artaud or Berkoff. Choices do not necessarily have to come from play scripts, but could be taken from famous speeches, for example. Whatever the selection, it is important that the extracts possess strong visual imagery and are not too abstract.

Exercise 4.9

➤ Approximately ten students form a circle, standing a metre apart. You are blindfolded and enter the centre of the circle. As in the exercise above you walk to the edge of the circle and are pushed back. After a degree of trust has been established, the circle provokes you more strongly – pulling and pushing, lifting you in the air, rolling you on the floor. At those points of most extreme provocation begin to speak your text, while continuing to be pushed and pulled by the circle. As the blindfolded person in the centre, you never know what will happen next – will you be lifted, pulled, rolled? You have no choice but to submit and accept. Thus the text is triggered and driven by the unforeseen pushes and pulls in a space that cannot be controlled.

➤ *First development* . . . : The actual physical provocations cease and – still wearing the blindfold – *imagine* you are being pulled, pushed, rolled and lifted as before. You move *as if* still being manipulated by members of the circle and, when ready, begin to say your text. At a certain pointing during this stage of the exercise the tutor may remove the blindfold.

➤ *Second development* . . . : Now you no longer move in the space, but speak the text as if the physical provocations are continuing. Thus the rhythms and cadences of the spoken text are still driven by those external forces of being pushed and pulled, rolled or lifted, etc. The observer continues to receive an impression that forces stronger than yourself are provoking you.

Exercise 4.10

➤ This exercise deepens the experience of being pulled or pushed and extends the challenge of embodying the words of the text. Here, tutor and students try to discover the corporeal dynamic of selected words in any given text, not through literary analysis, but by exploring the physical properties of the words, so as to create a *body memory* that can be later retrieved. Now you are pulled or pushed by the dynamics of particular words within the text. The main purpose of this exercise is that, once the overt physicalisation of the words becomes embedded in your body, when the text is spoken again without such extreme movements, the words will create an emotion that will *charge* the space and change its dynamic. If successful, this will be experienced by both actor and audience.

Exercise 4.11

➤ This final exercise applies the sensation of being pulled or pushed to the work of the chorus. Here, the voice of the individual is not important. It is the voice of the chorus which must be heard. This time, you should experience the power of the choral voice where you no longer speak as an individual. *You are spoken* – someone else speaks through you.

➤ Working in pairs, face your partner. One starts to speak a choral text. After a while, the other takes the words from his partner and also starts to speak. Shortly you are speaking the text together with the same rhythm, cadence and volume. You become one voice.

➤ *First development* . . . : Still in pairs, one of you stands directly behind the other. The one behind starts to whisper the text phrase by phrase. After the delivery of each phrase, allow a pause, so the person in front can repeat the piece of text just spoken. The student who repeats should try to echo the text, but with a loud voice. Through his voice, he gives a body to words that only he can hear, making visible the invisible.

➤ *Second development* . . . : As above, you stand behind your partner, but this time leaving a bigger space than before. Again, you whisper the text which is echoed by your partner in front. After a while, a third person positions himself behind you and starts to whisper the text. Now the two of you in front begin to echo the new whispering voice. A fourth person steps into the space, positions himself behind the third and begins to whisper the text which is echoed by the three in front. Then a fifth, a sixth . . . until fifteen students are in the space, giving voices to the text.

I PUSH MYSELF . . . I PULL MYSELF: TOWARDS THE DYNAMICS OF *COMMEDIA DELL'ARTE*

PHYSICAL PREPARATION

Exercise 4.12

➤ The tutor prepares a space full of obstacles for the students. This will be a kind of theatrical 'assault course' over which you must climb, crawl, jump, roll, swing and find a balance. Working in teams of six or seven, the groups will compete with each other to achieve the fastest time across the course. Tackling this course of obstacles should be a *playfully* competitive experience. In designing the assault course it is important to ensure that the students are exposed to physical sensations like pulling themselves up a wall or rope, pushing themselves through a tube or under a carpet, etc.

Exercise 4.13

➤ You are asked to analyse as precisely as possible a number of selected activities like ice skating, swimming (breaststroke), climbing up a rock face or crawling through a small tunnel. Here, the purpose is to understand in more depth the dynamics of pushing or pulling yourself. How do you move on ice, or in water in order to propel yourself forward? How do you pull and push yourself up the vertical cliff of a mountain? Which muscles are particularly used and in what sequence? What angles and shapes does your body produce during each of these activities?

Exercise 4.14

➤ This exercise connects the physical experience of pulling or pushing yourself with possible emotional states. As a 'safety barrier' students should line the sides of the studio. One by one, you are invited simply to cross the space and to note the sensations that are induced. Then each of you does the same again, but this time with eyes firmly closed. Compared to travelling with eyes open, you will feel a slight resistance in your bodies. This experience of resistance will become much greater when, for a third time, you have to cross the space, but on this occasion you must run with eyes closed. You have to push yourself to overcome your fear.

IMPROVISATION

The Awakening (neutral mask)

Half the group works on the improvisation, while the others observe:

You are asked to imagine that you awake for the first time surrounded by the wild natural world – a forest, a desert, a glacier, a mountain valley, etc. You start on the floor asleep, wake up slowly opening your eyes, and rise to look at the world in which you have mysteriously found yourself. You can begin to move around and experience this world physically and sensually. No anecdotes . . . no stories . . . no acting.

The Escape (neutral mask)

The improvisation may be done individually or in small groups:

Imagine yourself to be imprisoned in a tiny cell. You have made the decision to escape. You discover a means of breaking out of your cell, but then have to run down long corridors in search of a way out of the prison. You might be discovered by guards at any moment, so have to be very careful in your search. Finally, you find a door that leads into a large open space, and in the distance can see the perimeter wall that surrounds the prison. To reach the wall you must cross this space, which is patrolled by guards and searchlights. Despite the danger, you take the decision and run as fast as you can towards the wall. You reach the wall, scale it and jump to freedom down the other side.

This theme of escape exposes you to a situation of urgency in which you must overcome your fear to find freedom. You must push yourself to overcome all the obstacles that lie in the way.

Tutor notes

Both improvisations are ideally played with a neutral mask and confront the student with the necessity of breaking away from a situation that limits and constrains his entire energy. Whereas in *The Awakening* he breaks away from the unconscious world of dreams to push his body against the laws of gravity towards the vertical in order to discover the world, in *The Escape* he has to push himself against real obstacles. He discovers the necessity to push and pull himself in order to move on. Within these themes, often explored at Lecoq's school, the driving force is the deep desire for survival and to live. Here students must pull or push themselves to overcome obstacles.

INTO THE DRAMATIC TERRITORIES: *COMMEDIA DELL'ARTE*

Exercise 4.15

➤ Initially work in pairs. Take your partner's hand and pull him through the space. Now stand behind your partner trying to push him. In both cases your partner resists: he does not wish to be pulled or pushed. However, the one who is pushed or pulled should not resist to the point where there is immobility between the two. You should both travel through the space. In the second part of this exercise, small themes may be added to provide a dramatic element. For example, a parent who is trying to convince a child playing with his friends to come home, since it is already past his bedtime.

IMPROVISATION

The Divorce

Here, the theme introduced above is taken even further:

> Remain together as a pair, but identify yourselves as A and B. Partner A tries to
> pull or push partner B back home from the pub, since B's wife/husband is wait-
> ing. B, who does not want to go home, disputes with A, while A continues to pull
> or push him. The more A pushes or pulls, the more B resists. In exasperation,
> A tells B that the wife/husband at home is sick of his drinking habits and is think-
> ing of leaving. At first B does not believe this, but slowly gets very angry and
> decides that he will immediately return home to tell his partner that he wants a
> divorce. A tries to calm B down, but he runs off leaving A alone in the pub.

Tutor notes

This exercise is an introduction into the world of *commedia*, where the
stock characters change their moods – and decisions – from one instant
to the next. One moment the *commedia* character is pushed or pulled –
as with B above, who does not want to go home from the pub – but the
next moment they pull or push themselves as a result of some changed
circumstance, or new piece of information.

The Reconciliation

This theme is a development from the improvisation above, but is
performed in a group:

> A group of friends tries to reconcile a young husband and wife after their first
> big argument. Since they will not talk to each other any more, the friends
> have to try to convince the couple to start communicating with each other
> again. At one end of the studio a group are trying to convince the young woman,
> and at the other end another group are doing a similar job on the young
> man. After a while both are slowly persuaded by their friends and decide to
> meet each other. Somewhat reluctantly they walk towards each other, only
> to decide at the last moment to turn around and walk back, since they are
> not yet ready to forgive. Their friends continue to try to persuade them, but

this time with stronger arguments. The young man and woman attempt another reunion, but at the last moment cannot go through with it. The procedure is repeated several times until the friends are completely exhausted, fed up and have lost all hope of a possible reconciliation. However, unexpectedly, the two cannot hold back their love for each and the story ends with a tearful embrace.

Tutor notes

This situation should allow students to analyse very precisely each moment within the scene. When is someone pushed or pulled, and at what point does a character begin to push or pull himself? How can the actor translate these emotional movements into gestures? When working on *commedia*, the student will discover that these are the patterns inherent in the structure of this theatrical form. These are the typical behaviour patterns of *commedia* characters.

For example, Pantalone will push himself down to the floor to pretend that he is dead, in order that he can avoid paying off his debts, since he is a miser. The Captain will always push himself forward to impress a lady with his adventures and his bravery. However, we are never sure if he is telling the truth, since he is terribly vain. While the Captain pushes himself forward in order to pretend that he is a fearless hero, he is at the same time pulled back by his enormous fear, since he will run away the moment he sees a mouse.

All the main *commedia* characters are exposed to these kinds of opposing forces within themselves. This is the essential movement dynamic which needs to be found when playing *commedia*.

DEBRIEF

Depending on circumstances and context, tutors will wish to organise different levels of evaluation and debriefing with their students. All of you, however, should be invited to identify the main principles at work throughout the sequences you have experienced. It may be useful to talk openly about what effect the work has had on your bodies, rather than restricting the debrief to intellectual analysis alone. If time allows, further activities could be devised using the same principles, and the work could be put into practice by making productions – full-length or short extracts – from existing melodramatic or tragic texts. Equally, you could devise short *commedia* scenarios that attempt to build on what you have learned from the third section above. Finally, you should all reflect on what the experience of working through these exercises has done for your wider perceptions of drama and theatre.

5

CONCLUSION

The body knows things we don't yet know. But we must not speak too soon.
That's why we begin with silence to grasp better what we should say afterwards. It's essential to recover that silence which gives rise to speech.

(Lecoq, in Roy and Carasso 1999)

The body 'knowing before we know' is one of those logical paradoxes
that Lecoq clearly enjoyed. There are others to be found in *The Moving
Body*, but this comment in particular seems to provide an elegant
summation of so much of what his teaching embodied and stood
for. Given that he must have spoken these words shortly before his
death in 1999, they could also offer a fair epitaph for his working life.
The words are interesting, not simply because they neatly represent
the kernel of Lecoq's philosophy, but also – for someone with little
knowledge of how he taught – they might seem to signify that kind
of semi-mystical conundrum so beloved by rather fey, other-worldly
gurus and soothsayers. Lecoq was neither fey nor prone to soothsaying,
but within his thinking and daily practice there were certainly paradoxes, creative tensions and – some would argue – contradictions
(Figure 5.1). He was aware of many of these 'creative tensions': they
are not hidden deep in the texts of his work only to be revealed by
some awkward critic or academic probing for discrepancies in his
thinking. Indeed, in much of his writing, these paradoxes are presented

Figure 5.1
Jacques
Lecoq in
class (1998)

so as to be an essential part of any piece of analysis or commentary. Sometimes they add a touch of self-deprecation to an insight, but often they speak of an openness and refusal to accept that a debate or proposition needs 'closure' in order for it to be intellectually respectable. Sometimes, too, there is a playfulness in the articulation of an idea, when, for example, at the end of a long passage which extols and explains the virtues of the neutral mask as a teaching tool, he concedes that 'absolute and universal neutrality . . . is merely a temptation' (Lecoq 2000: 20).

The tensions and paradoxes that surface regularly, either in his own writing or in conversations I have had with people connected to Lecoq, focus upon the following kinds of relationships:

- The particular and the universal
- The practical and the 'poetic'
- Discipline and creativity
- Tradition and invention
- Romanticism and realism.

Many of these issues have already been rehearsed in different parts of this book, but perhaps the main point to be made here is that these dualisms, as Mark Evans put it to me in conversation, 'almost neatly sum up the tensions of the twentieth century' (Evans 2002). Within his own very particular territory of preparing students to make theatre, Lecoq inevitably is shadowing some of the major cultural debates of his time. How could it be otherwise for an institution with the breadth of vision and aspiration as that possessed by the Paris school? It is a measure, too, of Lecoq's unwillingness ever to fix his pedagogy into a *method* that could be reproduced as a formula for any student in any context. Given his constant stress on *preparation*, rather than the inculcation of *technique*, it is to be expected that there would be a degree of fluidity to both his precepts and daily practice. Or, to put it another way, given that the pedagogy and research methods of this one time sportsman and physiotherapist turned actor, director and theatre teacher were driven by practice and experiment, then it is almost inevitable that there would be flexibility and a lack of rigidity in his approach. On the receiving end of his teaching, students were often aware of this, as Andy Crook observes:

> I think there were contradictions there. You just had to go along with that. He
> could come in one day and say one thing, and the next day something totally
> different. But somehow it all made sense because I felt he was genuinely living
> in the moment. . . . The course was very structured, but I loved that mutability
> in Lecoq in that he kept changing what he taught. He had to see what was vital
> and what made sense at the time. But he was fun. He was *wicked*.
>
> (Crook 2002)

And yet, of course, there seems to be a tension between this sense of mutability in his daily teaching and a willingness to speak often and passionately of 'universal laws of theatre', of a 'common poetic deposit', or of a 'universal poetic sense'. It is Lecoq's readiness to use words like 'universal' or 'common' that, in some quarters, make him sound old-fashioned and out of kilter with a contemporary spirit that acknowledges only *relative* values. It is important to emphasise here that Lecoq does not lay claim to having invented 'universal' laws of theatre, rather to have rediscovered and re-presented them. In relation to 'poetic' he says that 'the word *poetic* is there precisely to show there are things we cannot define. Things which only poetry can define, that is what is between words, what's invisible' (Roy and Carasso 1999). When Lecoq speaks of theatre's 'universal laws', he is acknowledging, on the one hand, the traditions and historical conventions upon which his teaching is based, and, on the other, a belief that it is impossible to approach physical work in theatre without a set of principles upon which to construct creative practice, and a method for analysing and evaluating that practice. Again, this juxtaposition between the indefinable and transcendent qualities of an invisible poetry lying in the gaps 'between words', and apparently immutable 'universal laws', suggests at least a playful tension between two very different ways of understanding or explaining the world.

Some commentators find this kind of language a barrier when trying to understand and embrace Lecoq's work. John Keefe, for example, is concerned that the strength of Lecoq's teaching strategy around movement and the body becomes dissipated and distracted by what he regards as the 'purple prose' quality of Lecoq's writing. For Keefe:

> [when] really important ideas like stillness and neutrality get dressed up in
> overblown prose Lecoq becomes guilty of an excessive romanticism. . . .
> There's no need to dress it all up as some kind of muse of movement. He's

(Keefe 2002)

If Keefe's point was simply a criticism of Lecoq's use of language, then
it would be unimportant. However, what he is saying is that Lecoq
weakens what is otherwise a strong case by making larger and grander
claims for the significance of his discoveries than is necessary. As a
teacher of undergraduate students, Keefe will happily use and – as he
puts it – 're-contextualise' a number of Lecoq's exercises and insights.
Nonetheless, he is wary of embracing the dualism which proposes an
'experience versus innocence' dichotomy, and which affirms a kind of
pre-conscious purity over the consciousness of 'a cluttered adult world'
(Keefe 2002). Ex-Lecoq student, Andy Crook, might accept some of
Keefe's arguments, but does not feel that these points substantially
undermine the strength of Lecoq's work. Crook comments that 'at
its worst there was a level of romanticism, and I always found that
fascinating with Lecoq. But that's the tradition he came from – directly
back to Copeau. To a degree I think he was based in a world that was
of another age' (Crook 2002). All this points to that tension already
highlighted in Lecoq's work, namely the pull of tradition's roots on the
one hand and, on the other, a restless desire to discover, to keep
changing and to be aware of the demands of the present. Keefe
summarises the status of his own reservations like this: 'at its best it is
a tension, because tensions can become productive. At its worst it is a
misguided contradiction' (Keefe 2002).

In many ways, to call this section of the book 'a conclusion' is
unhelpful and misleading. The word seems to suggest a sense of closure
to the narrative of Lecoq's life and work. Although he has been dead
for over three years, the Paris school continues, as do others across
Europe and North America that are ready to invoke his name, so as to
illustrate the shape and direction of their teaching. Without ever
wanting to provide a detailed inventory of every aspect of Lecoq's
curriculum, this book has sought to capture the main principles, qualities and creative tensions in his thinking and daily practice at the Paris
school. I have examined how Lecoq taught, and what the main issues
of substance were that his curriculum – with both its *permanences* and
its restlessness – engaged with. I have argued that the *how* and *what* of

his teaching are intertwined and should only be separated for the schematic purposes of trying to understand better. In a way, as Lecoq himself pointed out, if the school trained actors it was almost as an afterthought, or as a by-product of its main activity, which was to investigate the corporeal basis of creativity. In this exploration, the five thousand or more students who have so far passed through the Paris school were Lecoq's – temporary – partners and co-researchers into a range of subject areas concerned with art, life and theatre, but all linked by the presence of the body and its movement in space. It is significant that, while his teaching and research had to be institutionalised into something called an *International School of Theatre*, Simon McBurney suggests that it was, in fact, 'more like a kind of art school in its breadth and range of interest and observation' (1994: 19). In various conversations Thomas Prattki made a similar point, saying that Lecoq was strongly influenced by the ideal of the Bauhaus and regularly reiterated that his school was not 'an acting school' and that he was merely *un collectionneur des gestes* ('a collector of gestures').

Although Lecoq's school is now often thought of as having made a major contribution to the rise of what, since the late 1970s has been called 'physical theatre', it is important to recall that he spent much of his life working against the grain and as an 'unorthodox outsider' (Bradby 2002b: 89). This hardly troubled Lecoq and, indeed, one senses that he would have been profoundly uneasy had he been offered the potentially stifling embrace of any theatre establishment, whether in France or further afield. Regardless of how one might evaluate his cultural status – Lecoq would have been indifferent to the task – there can be little doubt that he has had a major influence on some of the most exciting theatre projects of the last forty years.

In a book of polemical essays entitled *theatre@risk*, Michael Kustow surveys the contemporary theatre landscape in Britain and the West, arguing that, despite the commodification of theatre and the threat to live performance from the world of digital technology, theatre will always matter and have something essential to say about the 'age we have left and the age we are entering' (Kustow 2000: cover). In his book, which is only partly a lament, Kustow identifies a very small number of theatre artists, companies or productions that he regards as having been crucial to theatre's renewal over the last four decades. Lecoq's teaching has directly or indirectly influenced most of these examples: Théâtre de Complicité, Ariane Mnouchkine and Théâtre du

Soleil, **Robert Lepage** (1957–) and Julie Taymor. This account has already focused in some detail on one of Théâtre de Complicité's productions, but what is significant about this list is that these four names represent a wide continuum of theatre practice from the highly commercial production of *The Lion King*, directed by Taymor, and into which the Disney Corporation reputedly invested $10 million, to the politics of collaborative practice represented by Théâtre du Soleil. However, although there is much that differentiates these four examples, what they share between themselves *and* with Lecoq is a commitment to a vision of theatre in which the visual and movement qualities of performance are paramount.

There remain unanswered questions, though, as to the extent and depth of his dream for the 'theatre of tomorrow'. How broad was this vision? Would it have encompassed and affirmed the often detached and ironic non-linear fragmented constructions of postmodern performance? Would he have applauded the best work from the stables of Forced Entertainment or The Worcester Group? That inheritors of Lecoq's legacy have recently created work such as *Mnemonic* (Théâtre de Complicité) and *The Far Side of the Moon* (Robert Lepage), which embraces at least some of these qualities, suggest that the gap is less wide than certain critics might have us believe. Perhaps the key to such speculation lies in the presence or absence of 'play' in this kind of performance work that lies so close to live or performance art. When play is an ever-present dynamic, as it surely is in the most effective examples of performance, then Lecoq might perhaps have acknowledged the inventiveness and skilfulness of such practice. This debate, however, must remain unresolved in the pages of this book.

Because Lecoq was primarily a teacher and because he refused to propose a *method* or a *system* which had to be accepted in its entirety or not at all, his legacy will continue to be an open one, in which his ideas and practices are regularly given new life and different shape and are re-contextualised according to the circumstances of time and place. Rather than handing down the vocabulary of theatre that he constructed with his students for over forty years as 'tablets of stone', it is proper that those who wish to use his ideas do so not with an awed reverence, but in a playful relationship that can accommodate *les permanences* with *movement*. One imagines that Lecoq would have found this quite acceptable:

He was a very interesting man, very perceptive, very intelligent, very know-
ledgeable, but very composed. He was everything you did expect, but also
everything you didn't. I remember arriving at the school and expecting a very
fey and elegant mime teacher. But here was this big man . . . very French and
incredibly nimble – he could do things which even some of the acrobats
couldn't do.

(Evans 2002)

NAME GLOSSARY

The following glossary provides brief biographical details of figures – largely from the world of theatre – who have been cited in the book. It does not include better-known names like Stanislavsky, Artaud and Brecht, assuming the reader's acquaintance with such figures. It also excludes people who, although not well known – Amleto Sartori and Étienne Decroux, for example – have had their work discussed within the main body of the text.

Eugenio Barba (1936–)   Founder and director of the Odin Teatret since 1964, having trained with Jerzy Grotowski in Poland in the early 1960s. Barba's practice has been strongly influenced by Eastern forms of dance and drama and his productions tend to foreground the ritualistic, visual and movement dimensions of theatre.

Jean-Louis Barrault (1910–94)   As a young man he worked with Antonin Artaud, and between 1931 and 1933 trained and researched into the nature of mime with Étienne Decroux. In 1946 he created the Compagnie Renaud-Barrault with his actress wife, Madeleine Renaud. Barrault was resident director at many of Paris's leading theatres, including the Odéon and the Théâtre du Rond Point. His most famous performance was as the mime artist Duburau in Marcel Carné's film *Les Enfants du Paradis* in 1945. Myra Felner suggests that

Barrault's theory was 'a unique combination of the mysticism of Artaud, the techniques of Decroux and Dullin's concept of sincerity' (Felner 1985: 88).

Peter Brook (1925–)   In the 1950s and 1960s Brook was one of Britain's leading theatre directors. Although applauded for his innovative productions of, for example, *King Lear*, *Marat / Sade*, *Oedipus* and *A Midsummer Night's Dream*, Brook left London for Paris in 1970. Here he established his company in an old vaudeville theatre at the Bouffes du Nord and founded the International Centre of Theatre Research. Much of Brook's career has been in search of a universal language of theatre and his company has been resolutely multiracial. An enduring interest in myth has been expressed in such productions as the ten-hour stage adaptation of the Hindu *Mahabharata* in 1985.

Joseph Chaikin (1935–)   Chaikin trained and worked as a method actor before wholeheartedly rejecting its principles as being too narrow and dogmatic. In 1959 he joined the legendary Living Theater company led by Julian Beck and Judith Malina, but in 1963 formed his own company – the Open Theater – with seventeen young actors and four writers. His work has always focused on the collaborative process and has sought to explore new and different relationships between sound, word and movement imagery in performance. Chaikin's investigations into acting – encapsulated in his book, *The Presence of an Actor* (1972) – do not represent a system as such, but are an excitingly eclectic montage of thoughts, dreams, ideas and images, all designed to unleash the actor's imagination and creativity.

Léon Chancerel (1886–1965)   One of Copeau's select group, Les Copiaus, Chancerel was a playwright and director. He formed a professional touring company – Les Comédiens Routiers – in the 1930s and often made work for children through Le Théâtre de l'Oncle Sébastien. Chancerel was part of a broad anti-fascist theatre movement, but one based on religious rather than Marxist principles. His practice often drew heavily on Copeau's ideas and Chancerel was interested in reinventing the *commedia dell'arte* for modern audiences. Today, a biennial prize in his name is awarded for exceptional plays for children.

Michael Chekhov (1891–1955)   Nephew of playwright Anton Chekhov, Michael Chekhov trained initially with Stanislavsky but was soon to break with this tradition. Strongly influenced by the radical educationalist, Rudolph Steiner, Chekhov's approach to actor training focused on creativity and the use of the imagination to physicalise a role. After 1918 Chekhov came out strongly against Stanislavsky's use of personal experience and emotion, arguing that this was an essentially conservative strategy as it failed to encourage or release the actor's creativity. In the 1930s Chekhov worked at Dartington College in Devon, but on the outbreak of war moved to the USA, at first to Connecticut and then to Los Angeles. By the end of his life Chekhov had constructed a rigorous approach to acting, at the centre of which lay a preoccupation with creativity and imagination. This approach is encapsulated in the 1991 edition of his book *On the Technique of Acting*.

Gabriel Cousin (1918–)   With Lecoq, Cousin was one of a small band of anti-fascist theatre practitioners – Les Aurochs – who spent the final months of the Occupation in hiding and developing their skills in mime, dance and sport. After the war, Lecoq was to direct many of Cousin's plays. Committed to the idea of a popular and decentralised theatre, Cousin's plays engaged with social and political themes from an ethical standpoint. Although as a young man he was strongly influenced by Barrault, Cousin's work falls largely within the mainstream of post-war French theatre.

Dalcroze *see* **Jaques-Dalcroze**

Jean Dasté (1904–94)   A French actor and director who worked with Copeau's company in Burgundy, Dasté later joined Michel Saint-Denis's Compagnie des Quinze. With Copeau, he was a leading advocate of a decentralised popular theatre which might escape the constraints of Paris's hothouse and elitist atmosphere. After the war, he was a member of an influential group of theatre practitioners – including Lecoq – who saw theatre at least partly as a political project that would help emancipate the working class. To this end he was director of the Comédie de St Étienne from 1947 until 1970.

René Descartes (1596–1650)   Descartes's thought and writing have – for better or worse – exerted an enduring influence on our ideas about human nature. A central aspect of his philosophical thought was that the mind as a thinking substance was entirely distinct from the body. In the twentieth century many philosophers such as Gilbert Ryle and Ludwig Wittgenstein have challenged this notion of the 'ghostly mind' operating within a mechanical body. To accept Descartes' dualism between mind and body has major implications for our understanding of identity, the nature of human action and how we learn and survive in the world.

Charles Dullin (1885–1949)   An actor, director and producer, Dullin was very influential on the development of French theatre from the 1920s. A member of Copeau's troupe at the Le Vieux Columbier, he in turn trained artists such as Artaud and Barrault. He had a vision of theatre that was not concerned simply with mirroring reality; rather, that it should be an art form with its own internal poetic laws, standing apart from society and in which the power of imagination was the driving force. He became director of the Comédie Française in 1936.

Tim Etchells (1962–)   Etchells is a founder member and director of Sheffield-based performance ensemble, Forced Entertainment. Widely regarded as Britain's foremost experimental theatre company, Forced Entertainment was launched in 1984. The company makes provocative and challenging work that breaks – and plays – with the conventions of traditional theatre, particularly exploring the experience of urban Britain at the turn of the twentieth and twenty-first centuries. Etchells' own writing blends storytelling with criticism, the intimate with the global, and the fantastical with the mundane banalities of daily life.

Jerzy Grotowski (1933–99)   Grotowski was a Polish director and theatre-maker to whom the phrase 'poor theatre' is usually attributed. After training at the Krakow Theatre School, he established his own laboratory where he pioneered new ways of using movement and speech. His theatre productions explored myth and ritual and were often challengingly physical. Artaud and Stanislavsky were among his most important influences and, in turn, he was to have a major effect on some of Peter Brook's earlier productions, and also on the practice of The Living Theatre from North America. He disbanded his theatre laboratory in 1976 and much of his later work became a private and personal exploration.

Georges Hébert (1875–1957)   Hébert is a significant, but relatively unknown, figure in the twentieth-century history of movement training for the sportsperson and the performer. His influence can be traced via Copeau into the work of both Decroux and Lecoq. An officer in the French navy, Hébert revolutionised an approach to physical training in the armed forces. He studied the economical movements of the 'topmen' who sailed on the last fully rigged ships and his training methods – in contrast to the dominant 'Swedish Drill' (bodybuilding in our terms) of the time – proposed that the guiding principle should be one of rigorous physical economy of movement. In other words, in their training regimes athletes should aim to find exactly the right amount of energy – no more, no less – for the task prescribed. At his school, Copeau became convinced by this paradigm and replaced Dalcroze's rhythmic method with Hébert's 'utilitarian' exercises. The economy and simplicity of movement that Lecoq searches for in the neutral mask finds its origins in the radical thinking and experimentation of Hébert.

Émile Jaques–Dalcroze (1865–1950)   Dalcroze's system of eurhythmics enjoyed a great vogue in the period between the two world wars. His philosophy was that all actors should learn rhythmic dancing to improve their coordination and to help synchronise bodily movements with speech. He believed that every gesture and facial expression should serve to articulate an 'inner voice' and much of his work focused on the emotions aroused by musical rhythms. Copeau was initially very influenced by Dalcroze.

Louis Jouvet (1887–1951)   An actor and director who had collaborated with Copeau at Le Vieux Columbier, Jouvet became an influential figure in French theatre between the wars. Although much of his work was text-based, he was sceptical that naturalism could ever be an effective vehicle for theatre. Jouvet was particularly renowned for bringing Molière, Giradoux and Genet to the stage.

Robert Lepage (1957–)   Lepage trained at the Conservatoire d'Art Dramatique in Quebec, where he was exposed to the principles of Lecoq's teaching and approach to theatre. Impossible to categorise, Lepage is an actor, director, writer and film-maker whose work has often been formally innovative and multidisciplinary. He has particularly explored the use of modern technologies to redefine the parameters between theatre, film and live art. His most challenging work has included *Tectonic Plates* (1988), *Needles and Opium* (1991), *Seven Streams of the River Ota* (1994) and *The Far Side of the Moon* (1999).

Marcel Marceau (1923–)   Marceau came to Paris during the Second World War to train at Charles Dullin's Atelier. There he became a student of Étienne Decroux, who taught him the technical base – the grammar – of illusionary mime, which he was to perfect and perform for the rest of his life. Later, Decroux was to reject this popular application of his training and the two became distant. Marceau worked with Barrault after the war and shared with him a desire to reach the public – a strategy in which Decroux showed little interest. Marceau's most famous characterisation has been Bip, a white-faced clown descended from the tradition of Pierrot. He founded his own mime school in Paris in 1978 that – coincidentally – lies only a short distance from Lecoq's own establishment on the rue du Faubourg St Denis.

Vsevolod Meyerhold (1874–1940)   Meyerhold was a Russian actor and director who, although a lifelong friend and colleague of Stanislavsky, broke sharply away from the traditions of naturalism, proposing instead a strongly visual and physical theatre that aimed to fire the imagination rather than mimic real life. He was a prolific director of productions, an innovative teacher and a theorist of the avant garde. In 1921, he became director of the Moscow State Higher Theatre Workshop and perfected a system of physical training for the actor called 'Biomechanics'. During this period he was an enthusiastic supporter of the aims of the Bolshevik revolution and directed his theatrical and artistic energy towards serving this cause. However, by the mid-1930s he was attacked by Stalin's authorities and his theatre closed down. Despite the courageous support of Stanislavsky, Meyerhold and his wife were imprisoned and murdered in 1940. Since the 1960s, when his writing began to be translated into English, Meyerhold's reputation has been rehabilitated and he is now widely regarded as one of the greatest figures of twentieth-century theatre.

Ariane Mnouchkine (1939–)   A French director who founded the experimental theatre company, Le Théâtre du Soleil, in 1964, Mnouchkine studied psychology at the Sorbonne in 1959, but also trained with Jacques Lecoq between 1967 and 1968. The company's early work was committed to a socialist 'people's theatre', following the principles of Jean Vilar's Théâtre Nationale Populaire. By the 1970s, Mnouchkine had seen the work of Peter Brook and began to explore the principles and practice of inter-culturalism, both of them being influenced by Artaud. For Mnouchkine, however, a commitment to oriental theatre was not about resuscitating ancient theatrical forms for Western audiences, but more to do with reinventing the rules and principles of some of these forms for the contemporary world. Over the last twenty years, she has collaborated regularly with writer, philosopher and cultural theorist, Hélène Cixous.

Jean Renoir (1894–1979)   Renoir was a French film director, screenwriter and occasional actor, who is widely acknowledged as one of the 'giants' of world cinema. Many of his films combined a strong sense of poetry with a deep social and political commitment. Technically, he explored the use of long takes and deep-focus photography. Two of his most admired films – *La Grande Illusion* and *La Règle du Jour* – were made in the 1930s, the former a great anti-war statement, and the latter a scathing satire on French aristocratic society.

Jean-Jacques Rousseau (1712–78)   Rousseau came to be regarded as the prophet of the French Revolution and his political critiques of power, inequality and private property remained influential with radicals and romantics throughout the nineteenth century. However, he also believed that modern culture and society were prone to corruption and decay and, towards the end of his life, increasingly advocated ways of living which represented a return to an imagined simpler and more primitive past – a past that was more in tune with nature and the wonders of a natural universe. Innes in *Avant Garde Theatre* (1993) argues that much of the early twentieth-century avant-garde movement subscribed to Rousseau's ideas on the 'purity' and simplicity of nature.

Michel Saint-Denis (1897–1971)   A French director and actor who founded the London Theatre Studio (1936) and later the Old Vic School, he trained with his uncle – Jacques Copeau – at Le Vieux Columbier and then founded the celebrated Compagnie des Quinze in 1930. Much of his life was devoted to teaching and he became the main transmitter of Copeau's ideas in Britain and North America. Towards the end of his life he collaborated with the Royal Shakespeare Company, particularly on plays by Brecht.

Julie Taymor (1952–)   Born in Massachusetts, Taymor's work as a director, actor and designer of masks and puppets has spanned both the experimental and commercial ends of theatre. At sixteen she trained with Jacques Lecoq, from whom she gained an understanding of the actor's body as a 'complete resource' for theatre. All her work has been driven by an interest in investigating theatre forms from across the world that seek to fire the imagination, rather than aiming to mimic reality. Taymor's early work was the product of her research into myth and ritual and the forms of mask and puppet theatre to be found in Indonesia. In 1997, she was commissioned by Disney to produce and direct a theatre version of *The Lion King*. This highly commercial production managed to incorporate many of the experimental techniques from her early work in Java and Bali.

BIBLIOGRAPHY

BOOKS, JOURNALS AND INTERVIEWS

Auslander, Philip (1997) *From Acting to Performance*, London and New York: Routledge.

Barker, Paul (1994) 'Inside Story: Théâtre de Complicité', *Independent on Sunday*, London, 5 November.

Baudrillard, Jean (1970) *La Société de consummation*, Paris: Gallimard.

Berkoff, Steven (1999) 'Obituary of Jacques Lecoq', *Total Theatre* 11(1): 5.

Bradby, David (1984) *Modern French Drama 1940–1980*, Cambridge: Cambridge University Press.

—— (2002a) Unpublished interview with author, London, 23 May.

—— (2002b) 'Jacques Lecoq and his École Internationale de Théâtre in Paris', in David Bradby and Maria Delgado (eds) *The Paris Jigsaw: Internationalism and the City's Stages*, Manchester and New York: Manchester University Press.

Bührer, Michel (1984) *Mummenschanz*, Altstätten: Panorama Verlag.

Callery, Dymphna (2001) *Through the Body: A Practical Guide to Physical Theatre*, London: Nick Herne Books.

Chamberlain, Franc and Yarrow, Ralph (eds) (2002) *Jacques Lecoq and the British Theatre*, London and New York: Routledge.

Cocuzza, Ginnine (1979) 'Review of Mummenschanz', *Mime News* (May/June).

Counsell, Colin (1996) *Signs of Performance: An Introduction to Twentieth-century Performance*, London and New York: Routledge.

Croft, Susan (1992) 'Transforming Schulz', essay in programme for *The Street of Crocodiles*, London: Théâtre de Complicité.

Crook, Andy (2002) Unpublished interview with author, Dublin, 3 May.

Dasté, Jean (1977) *Voyage d'un comédien*, Paris: Stock.

Decroux, Étienne (1985) 'Words on Mime', trans. Mark Piper, in Thomas Leabhart, (ed.) *Mime Journal*, California: Pomona College Theatre Department.

De Marinis, Marco (1995) 'The Mask and Corporeal Expression in Twentieth Century Theatre', in Thomas Leabhart (ed.) *Mime Journal*, California: Pomona College Theatre Department, pp. 14–37.

Dennis, Anne (1995) *The Articulate Body: The Physical Training of the Actor*, New York: Drama Book Publishers.

Drijver, Rieks (1998) 'Theatre of the Imagination', *Total Theatre* 10(2): 14–15.

Eldredge, Sears A. and Huston, Hollis W. (1995 [1978]) 'Actor Training in the Neutral Mask', in Philip B. Zarrilli (ed.) *Acting (Re)Considered*, London and New York: Routledge, pp. 121–8.

Eldridge, John and Eldridge, Lizzie (1994) *Raymond Williams: Making Connections*, London and New York: Routledge.

Etchells, Tim (1995) *Play On: Collaboration and Process*, unpublished draft version presented in Wolverhampton, England.

—— (1999) *Certain Fragments: Contemporary Performance and Forced Entertainment*, London and New York: Routledge.

Evans, Mark (2002) Unpublished interview with author, Coventry, 9 July.

Featherstone, Mike, Hepworth, Mike and Turner, Bryan (eds) (1991) *The Body: Social Process and Cultural Theory*, London: Sage.

Felner, Mira (1985) *Apostles of Silence: The Modern French Mimes*, Cranberry and London: Associated University Presses.

Freshwater, Helen (2001) 'The Ethics of Indeterminacy: Théâtre de Complicité's *Mnemonic*', *New Theatre Quarterly* 67: 212–18.

Frost, Anthony and Yarrow, Ralph (1990) *Improvisation in Drama*, London: Macmillan.

Fulford, Robert (1988) 'Deep into Private Mythology with Bruno Schulz', *Globe and Mail*, Toronto, 22 July.

Gardner, Lyn (1997) 'The Face of the Future', *Guardian*, London, 19 November.

Garduño, Flor and Lyr, Guyette (1997) *Mummenschanz 1972–1997*, Altstätten: Tobler Verlag.

Hiley, Jim (1988) 'Moving Heaven and Earth: Interview with Jacques Lecoq', *Observer*, London, 20 March.

Hodge, Alison (ed.) (2000) *Twentieth Century Actor Training*, London and New York: Routledge.

Innes, Christopher (1993) *Avant Garde Theatre 1892–1992*, New York and London: Routledge.

Jameson, Fredric (1991) *Postmodernism, or the Cultural Logic of Late Capitalism*, London and New York: Verso.

Jenkins, Ron (2001) 'A Prophet of Gesture Who Got Theater Moving', *New York Times*, 18 March.

Johnson, Mark (1987) *The Body in the Mind: The Bodily Basis of Meaning, Imagination and Reason*, Chicago and London: University of Chicago Press.

Kalb, Jonathan (1989) *Beckett in Performance*, Cambridge and New York: Cambridge University Press.

Keefe, John (1995) 'Dramaturgy and Structure: Looking with Knowledge', *Total Theatre* 7(3).

—— (2002) Unpublished interview with author, London, 23 May.

Kustow, Michael (2000) *theatre@risk*, London: Methuen.

Leabhart, Thomas (1989) *Modern and Post-modern Mime*, London: Macmillan.

Lecoq, Fay (2001) Unpublished interview with author, Paris, 27 October.

Lecoq, Jacques (1973 [1972]) 'Mime – Movement – Theatre', trans. Kat Foley and Julia Devlin, *Yale Theatre* 4(1).

—— (1987) *Le Théâtre du geste*, trans. Gill Kester (2002), Paris: Bordas.

—— (2000) *The Moving Body*, trans. David Bradby, London: Methuen.

Lecoq, Pascale (2001) Unpublished interview with author, Paris, 26 October.

Lepage, Robert (1992) 'In Discussion with Richard Eyre', in *Platform Papers*, London: Royal National Theatre, pp. 23-41.

Marshall, Lorna (2001) *The Body Speaks*, London: Methuen.

McBurney, Simon (1992) Programme for *The Street of Crocodiles*, London: Théâtre de Complicité.

—— (1994) 'The Celebration of Lying', in David Tushingham (ed.) *Live: Food for the Soul*, London: Methuen, pp. 13–24.

—— (1999a) 'Obituary of Jacques Lecoq', *Guardian*, London, 23 January.

—— (1999b) 'Interview', in Gabriella Giannachi and Mary Luckhurst (eds) *On Directing: Interviews with Directors*, London: Faber and Faber, pp. 67–77.

McCaw, Dick (2002) Unpublished interview with author, London, 22 May.

McCullough, Christopher (ed.) (1998) *Theatre Praxis: Teaching Drama Through Practice*, London: Macmillan.

Milling, Jane and Ley, Graham (2001) *Modern Theories of Performance: From Stanislavski to Boal*, Basingstoke and New York: Palgrave.

Mime Journal (1993/1994) 'Words on Decroux 1', Thomas Leabhart (ed.), Claremont, Calif.: Pomona College Theatre Department.

—— (1997) 'Words on Decroux 2', Thomas Leabhart (ed.), Claremont, Calif.: Pomona College Theatre Department.

Murray, Simon (2002) '*Tout bouge*: Jacques Lecoq, Modern Mime and the Zero Body', in Franc Chamberlain and Ralph Yarrow (eds) *Jacques Lecoq and the British Theatre*, London and New York: Routledge, pp. 17–44.

Pavis, Patrice (1998) *Dictionary of the Theatre: Terms, Concepts and Analysis*, trans. Christine Shantz, Toronto and London: University of Toronto Press.

Prattki, Thomas (2001) Unpublished interview with author, Paris, March.

—— (2002) Unpublished interview with author, Paris, 26 October.

Regan, Stephen (2000) 'Critical Theories and Performance: Introduction', in Lizbeth Goodman and Jane de Gay (eds) *Politics and Performance*, London and New York: Routledge, pp. 49–54.

Rolfe, Bari (1972) 'The Mime of Jacques Lecoq', *Drama Review* 16(1): 34–8.

—— (1974) 'Masks, Mime and Mummenschanz', in Thomas Leabhart (ed.) *Mime Journal* 2, Claremont, Calif.: Pomona College Theatre Department, pp. 1–6.

Romney, Jonathan (1999) 'Even Tables and Chairs have Souls', *Guardian*, London, 29 January.

Rudlin, John (2000) 'Jacques Copeau: The Quest for Sincerity', in Alison Hodge (ed.) *Twentieth Century Actor Training*, London and New York: Routledge, pp. 55–78.

Ruffini, Franco (1995) 'Mime, the Actor, Action: The Way of Boxing', in Thomas Leabhart (ed.) *Incorporated Knowledge: The Mime Journal*, Claremont, Calif.: Pomona College Theatre Department, pp. 54–69.

Sanchez-Colberg, Ana (1996) 'Altered States and Subliminal Spaces: Charting the Road Towards a Physical Theatre', *Performance Research* 1(2): 40–56.

Schulz, Bruno (1980) 'Interview with Bruno Schulz', in Stanislaw Ignacy Witkiewicz *Beelzebub Sonata: Plays, Essays, Documents*, ed. and trans. Daniel Gerould and Jadwiga Kosicka, New York: Performing Arts Journal Publications.

—— (1988) *The Fictions of Bruno Schulz: The Street of Crocodiles and Sanatorium under the Sign of the Hourglass*, London: Picador.

Schürch, Bernie and Frassetto, Floriana (2002) Unpublished interview with author, Biel, Switzerland, 22 June.

Shevtsova, Maria (1989) 'The Sociology of the Theatre, Part Two: Theoretical Achievements', *New Theatre Quarterly* 18: 180–94.

Shilling, Chris (1993) *The Body and Social Theory*, London: Sage Publications.

Sklar, Deirdre (1995) 'Étienne Decroux's Promethean Mime', in Philip Zarrilli (ed.) *Acting (Re)Considered*, London and New York: Routledge, pp. 108–20.

Taymor, Julie (1999) 'From Jacques Lecoq to *The Lion King*', *The Drama Review* 43(3) (T163): 36–55.

Théâtre de Complicité (1999) *The Street of Crocodiles*, London: Methuen.

Updike, John (1988) 'Introduction', in Bruno Schulz *The Fictions of Bruno Schulz: The Street of Crocodiles and Sanatorium under the Sign of the Hourglass*, London: Picador.

Valdez, Carolina (1999) 'Obituary of Jacques Lecoq', *Total Theatre* 11(1): 8.

Vidal, John (1988) 'Opening Moves: Interview with Jacques Lecoq', *Guardian*, London, 22 March.

Ward, Nigel (1996) ' "Théâtre Populaire": Ideology and Tradition in French Popular Theatre', in Ros Merkin (ed.) *Popular Theatres?*, Liverpool: Liverpool John Moores University, pp. 172–82.

Williams, David (ed.) (1999) *Collaborative Theatre: The Théâtre du Soleil Sourcebook*, London and New York: Routledge.

Williams, Raymond (1976) *Keywords*, London: Fontana.

—— (1989) *The Politics of Modernism*, London: Verso.

Wright, John (2002) 'The Masks of Jacques Lecoq', in Franc Chamberlain and Ralph Yarrow (eds) *Jacques Lecoq and the British Theatre*, London and New York: Routledge, pp. 71–84.

Zarrilli, Philip (ed.) (1995) *Acting (Re)Considered*, New York and London: Routledge.

VIDEOS

Kauz, Magdalena (2000) *Mummenschanz 1972–2000*, Altstätten: Mummenschanz Foundation.

The Late Show (1992) 'Théâtre de Complicité, profiled in rehearsal for *The Street of Crocodiles*', BBC2, September.

Musale, Kamal (2001) *Mummenschanz: The Musicians of Silence*, Altstätten: Mummenschanz.

Roy, Jean-Noël and Carasso Jean-Gabriel (1999) *Les Deux Voyages de Jacques Lecoq*, Paris: La Septe ARTE–On Line Productions–ANRAT.

INDEX

Bold type indicates illustrations.

eBooks – at www.eBookstore.tandf.co.uk

A library at your fingertips!

eBooks are electronic versions of printed books. You can store them on your PC/laptop or browse them online.

They have advantages for anyone needing rapid access to a wide variety of published, copyright information.

eBooks can help your research by enabling you to bookmark chapters, annotate text and use instant searches to find specific words or phrases. Several eBook files would fit on even a small laptop or PDA.

NEW: Save money by eSubscribing: cheap, online access to any eBook for as long as you need it.

Annual subscription packages

We now offer special low-cost bulk subscriptions to packages of eBooks in certain subject areas. These are available to libraries or to individuals.

For more information please contact webmaster.ebooks@tandf.co.uk

We're continually developing the eBook concept, so keep up to date by visiting the website.

www.eBookstore.tandf.co.uk